Bible Basics:

Lessons for Life

An Overview of God's Word

Phyllis Vos Wezeman

Dedication

To Ann and Ron Liechty,

Who have helped me to explore God's Word and to learn

lessons that are basic for life. (P. V. W.)

SPECIAL THANKS TO:

Katherine Robinson Coleman for illustrating this resource.

Ken Wezeman for providing technical and theological support!

Illustrations by Katherine Coleman. Cover design by Karin Wilson.

BIBLE BASICS Lessons for Life: An Overview of God's Word

by Phyllis Vos Wezeman

Copyright © 2000 Educational Ministries, Inc.

ISBN 1-57438-040-0

Educational Ministries, Inc.

165 Plaza Dr, Prescott, AZ 86303

800-221-0910

Table Of Contents

Overview: Bible Basics — 7

What Is The Bible? — 9
- What is the Bible? — 9
- How did we get the Bible? — 11
- What are the parts of the Bible? — 14
- What are the books of the Bible? — 18
- Why is the Bible important? — 19

The Old Testament — 21
- Old Testament Review — 21
- Law — 24
- History — 25
- Poetry — 27
- Prophets — 28

The New Testament — 31
- New Testament Review — 32
- Gospels — 33
- History — 34
- Epistles — 35
- Prophecy — 36

Producing The Bible — 39
- Books Of The Bible Review — 39
- Language Systems — 40
- Writing Surfaces — 41
- Printing Processes — 43
- Translating Techniques — 44

Using The Bible — 47
- Versions Of The Bible — 47
- Book Names And Abbreviations — 50

● Book, Chapter And Verse   53
● Cross References   54
● Supplements   56

Studying The Bible   59
● Books Of The Bible Review   60
● Atlas   61
● Commentary   62
● Concordance   63
● Bible Dictionary   64

Sharing The Bible   67
● Dance Directions   67
● Memorized Messages   69
● Project Possibilities   70
● Story Spoons   72
● T-Shirt Themes   73

Enhancements   75

Supplements   77
● Chart Of The English Bible   77
● Intergenerational Learning   79
● Learning Activities Used In <u>Bible Basics</u>   81
● Learning Centers   85
● Learning Styles/Multiple Intelligences   86
● Lesson Planning   90
● Workshop Rotation Model   92

Resources   93

Foreword

The Danish philosopher, Soren Kierkegaard, wrote:

> "We shall read the Bible with personal concern,
> Realizing that it is not a textbook but a letter from
> God with your personal address on it."

As I travel the country in my position with the American Bible Society, I have become more and more aware of the Biblical illiteracy that inhabits our land! It is very difficult, if not impossible, for us to read the Bible with personal concern if we have no idea of how the Bible came to be or what the various books emphasize.

Phyllis Wezeman addresses these issues in this book. She is not nearly so concerned as to which denomination or group knows the most, but rather that each of us is empowered with the basics in order that we can read and study the Bible with personal concern.

John Wesley has some good advice for us too:

"I advise everyone, before he/she reads the Scripture, to use this or the like prayer:

> Blessed Lord, who has caused all holy Scriptures to be written for our learning, grant that we may in such wise hear them, read, mark, learn and inwardly digest them, that by patience and comfort of thy holy Word, we may embrace and ever hold fast the blessed hope of everlasting life, which thou hast given us in our Savior Jesus Christ."

May God's blessing be yours as you study the "Basics" and prepare yourself to read with personal concern this letter from God with your personal address on it!

Haviland C. Houston, Director
Resources for Christian Educators
American Bible Society

 # *Overview: Bible Basics*

How many people really know what's in the Bible? Two Testaments—Old and New... 66 books—39 in Part One and 27 in Part Two ... over 1100 Chapters ... more than 31,000 Verses ... nearly 775,000 words.[1] Studying God's Word is a lifelong process—and then even the best students of the Bible only scratch the surface.

Today there seems to be a renewed emphasis on Bible study. People want to know what's in the Bible. But, people want something more than facts; they want something that will help them understand the content and the key points of God's Word. And, they want something to help them apply this information to their lives. Bible Basics is an attempt to help teachers and students (and the writer too!) explore the content of the Bible in a simple, yet significant, way. Bible Basics is a series of lessons on God's Word as a whole as well as on each Book of the Old and New Testaments. Four books are projected in this series:

- Bible Basics: Lessons For Life— An Overview Of God's Word;

- Bible Basics: Lessons For Life— Genesis Through Esther;

- Bible Basics: Lessons For Life— Job Through Malachi;

- Bible Basics: Lessons For Life—Matthew Through Revelation.

Themes in Book One, Bible Basics: Lessons For Life — An Overview Of God's Word include:

- "What is the Bible?"
- "The Old Testament"
- "The New Testament"
- "Producing The Bible"
- "Using The Bible"
- "Studying The Bible"

- "Sharing The Bible".

Chapters in subsequent books—beginning with Genesis and ending with Revelation—will contain an introduction and five lessons including:

- **Sequence**—a review of the books of the Bible;
- **Statistics**—a project to provide basic information about the book;
- **Stories**—an activity related to key people and stories of the book;
- **Scripture**—a design to discover the message of the book's key verse;
- **Significance**—an exercise to emphasize the book's importance for God's people today.

Bible Basics is a valuable resource for anyone involved in the worship, education, outreach and nurture ministries of a congregation. Inviting, informing, involving learning activities are used to impart information and ideas. Lessons in the book may be used in Church School classes, Worship centers, Children's Church, Vacation Bible School sessions, Mid-week ministries, Kid's clubs, Intergenerational Events, Before and After School care programs, Youth Groups, Retreats, Confirmation Classes, as well as in day-schools and homes. The lessons are for people of all ages—children, youth and adults—but are especially designed for young people in elementary school with reading skills.

Provided in an easy-to-use format, each lesson lists the materials required for the project, offers directions for advance preparation, and gives complete procedures for accomplishing the task.

It is suggested that instruction takes place through involvement in a series of Learning Centers, however many other learning options are possible. Regardless of the design for individual, small or large group instruction, there must be a way to interest, to instruct, and to involve the participants; a way to explain, to explore, and to evaluate the lesson. For additional information about Learning Models and Lesson Planning see the "Supplements" Chapter of this resource.

Bible Basics is intended to help participants explore God's Word in creative, concrete and challenging ways, and to experience its message as a guide for life. May all who participate in this study of the Bible learn lessons from God's Word that are basic for life.

[1]Wilmington, H.L. Wilmington's Books of Lists. Wheaton, IL: Tyndale, 1987.

What Is The Bible?

Before beginning a study of each book of the Bible, it is important to answer some basic questions about the Bible as a whole. And, the most basic question might be "What is the Bible?" This chapter offers activities to address the topic in five ways:

- "What is the Bible?"
- "How did we get the Bible?"
- "What are the parts of the Bible?"
- "What are the books of the Bible?"
- "Why is the Bible important?"

Although learning information about the Bible is one purpose of participation in these lessons, there is a greater goal! What's really important is that each participant learn to use the information in the Bible to identify and understand God's plan for his or her own life.

What Is The Bible?

Activity

- Graffiti Chalkboard

Materials

- ☐ Bibles
- ☐ Scissors
- ☐ Heavy Cardboard, 8 1/2" x 11" pieces
- ☐ Concordance
- ☐ Chalk
- ☐ Facial tissues, paper towels, or rags
- ☐ Adhesive backed chalkboard plastic (available at hardware or variety stores)

Advance Preparation

- ☐ Cut heavy cardboard into 8 1/2" x 11" pieces (one per person).
- ☐ Cut adhesive backed chalkboard plastic pieces to fit one or both sides of the cardboard.

Method

"What is the Bible?" is a question that has been asked by countless people for thousands of years. And, it is a question that people still ask today. Although there are many ways to answer the question, the best response is that the Bible is the Word of God! Even though the contents of the sixty-six books were written by many authors over the span of 1000 - 2000 years, it is still God's Word. Though the writers used their own minds, hands, and tools, God inspired each person—in varied times and places—to write the message that God wanted to share—God is LOVE. The Bible is the collection of books recognized by the Christian Church as the inspired record of the revelation of God and of God's will.

One way to find answers to the question "What is the Bible?" is to turn to the source—Scripture itself. Begin this project by making a chalkboard to use to record key words and phrases about the Bible.

Select a piece of cardboard. Cover one or both sides of the cardboard with adhesive backed chalkboard plastic. Smooth the material while applying it to the cardboard to remove air bubbles and press hard so the adhesive adheres to the backing. Add brown utility tape to create a border around the chalkboard. Use white or colored chalk to write on the surface of the board. Facial tissues, paper towels, or "rags" make great erasers.

Once the board is prepared, print the words "WHAT IS THE BIBLE?" across the top of one side. Find answers to the question by looking up a variety of Scripture passages. Write a word or phrase about each reference—graffiti style—on the board. Old Testament Bible verses to use include: Psalm 91:4; Psalm 119:105; Isaiah 55:10-11; Jeremiah 23:29.

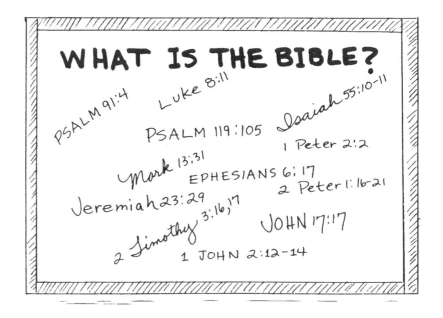

New Testament passages to review are: Mark 13:31; Luke 8:11; John 17:17; Ephesians 6:17; 2 Timothy 3:16,17; 1 Peter 2:2; 2 Peter 1:16-21; 1 John 2:12-14.

To find additional verses, look up "WORD," "WORD OF GOD," or "WORD OF THE LORD" in a concordance. Locate the Scripture references listed and add more ideas to the chalkboard.

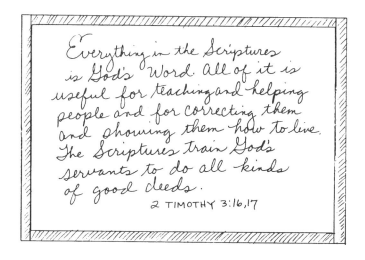

Turn the board over and write your favorite verse on the back—perhaps 2 Timothy 3:16,17— "Everything in the Scriptures is God's Word. All of it is useful for teaching and helping people and for correcting them and showing them how to live. The Scriptures train God's servants to do all kinds of good deeds." (CEV)

How Did We Get The Bible?

Activity

- Sequencing Sheets

Materials

- ❏ Sequencing Sheets
- ❏ Paper
- ❏ Clothesline
- ❏ Reference books (optional)

- ❏ Duplicating equipment
- ❏ Answer sheet
- ❏ Clip clothes pins

Advance Preparation

- ❏ Enlarge the "Sequencing Sheets" and duplicate several sets for the Learning Center or one set for each participant.

❑ Let participants know if they are to leave the "Sequencing Sheets" in the Learning Center or if they may take them home.

Method

In order to answer the question "How did we get the Bible?" it is helpful to put the events that took place over thousands of years into a simple sequence, that is—to put the events in the order in which they might have happened. Key words and descriptive phrases are provided for seven broad categories of the process. Read the information on the "Sequencing Sheets" and put the papers in the order in which the events might have occurred. Using clip clothes pins, attach the sheets to the clothesline in sequence. Although what is presented here is a logical order, in reality there is no absolutely correct order. For example, although the stories of the Bible were spoken before they were written, these events were probably going on at the same time in different places!

Check the answer sheet to compare another interpretation of the sequence. Although we can't be one-hundred percent sure what happened when, we can be sure that God guided the entire process so that God's will was communicated to people in all times and in all places.

Sequencing Sheets

Spoken

Before the words of the Bible were written, oral stories of the history of God's dealings with God's people were passed from generation to generation.

Written

Authors in various times and places were inspired by God to write down the stories of God and His people on whatever materials they had available.

Copied

Scribes made copies of the written texts so the words could be read by people in various places.

Translated

So the stories could be shared with people in their own language, the first major translation of the Old Testament from Hebrew to Greek was made and called the Septuagint.

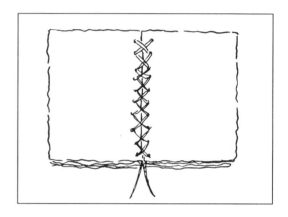

Read

As the books of the Bible were read over and over in synagogues and churches they became recognized as God's Word so that God's truth could be distinguished from false teachings.

Recognized

Several Councils, or official meetings of the church, acknowledged the 39 books of the Old Testament and the 27 books of the New Testament to be the inspired Word of God.

Affirmed

Ancient manuscripts discovered in caves along the Dead Sea in the 1940s confirmed the accuracy of the Biblical manuscripts.

Sequencing Sheets Answers

SPOKEN

WRITTEN

COPIED

TRANSLATED

CONFIRMED

AFFIRMED

READ

What Are The Parts Of The Bible?

Activity

- Crossword Puzzle

Materials

- ❑ Crossword Puzzle sheet
- ❑ Duplicating equipment
- ❑ Pencils or pens
- ❑ Dictionary

- ❑ Paper
- ❑ Answer sheet
- ❑ Bibles

Advance Preparation

- ❑ Enlarge the crossword puzzle and duplicate a copy for each participant.

Method

Try a crossword puzzle to learn more about the parts of the Bible. Read the material provided and have a Bible handy to look up information that will help answer the questions.

Although the Bible is considered to be one book, how many parts—called Testaments—does it contain? Two—the Old and the New. Originally, the Old Testament was written in the Hebrew language (with a few passages in Aramaic), and the New Testament was written in Greek. Look up the word "testament" in a dictionary. One of its meanings is "covenant." Look up the word covenant; it means agreement. Sometimes the Old Testament, the Hebrew Scripture, is called the "Old" covenant because it contains the stories of God's agreement to send the Messiah to save God's people from their sin. The New Testament is often called the "new" covenant, or the Christian Scriptures, because it tells the story of Jesus, the Savior.

Although the Bible is one book, with two main sections, it is actually a collection of 66 individual books—39 in the Old Testament and 27 in the New Testament. Bibles used in the Roman Catholic church, as well as some other faith traditions, contain 14 more books called the "Apocrypha"—books that were probably written between the testaments.

Although the Bible consists of 66 different books written over 1000 to 2000 years by many different people, it has a unity that can only be explained by acknowledging that the writers were inspired by the Holy Spirit to record God's message for all people. The theme of this message is the same in both Testaments: redemption. The Old Testament tells about the origin of sin and the preparation God made for the solution of this problem through the gift of His own Son the Messiah. The New Testament describes the fulfillment of God's redemptive plan through Jesus Christ. The Gospels tell of the Messiah's coming, Acts describes the origin and growth of the Church, and the Epistles teach the Church how to live the Good News.

Complete the crossword puzzle using this information and the Bible. Compare your responses to the answer sheet.

Parts of the Bible

Across	Down
1. Bible theme	2. First five books
6. N.T. language	3. O.T. books
8. N.T. books	4. Testament means...
10. Bible books	5. Old and New
12. Stories about Jesus	7. O.T. language
	9. Letters to churches
	11. Inspired by...

Parts of the Bible

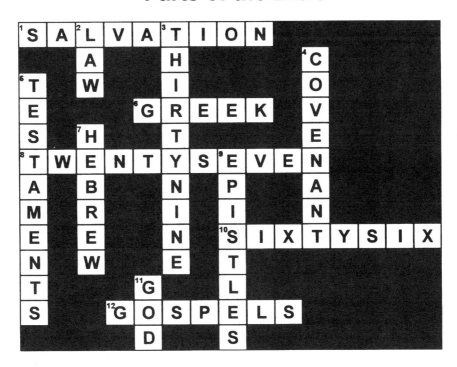

Across	Down
1. Bible theme	2. First five books
6. N.T. language	3. O.T. books
8. N.T. books	4. Testament means...
10. Bible books	5. Old and New
12. Stories about Jesus	7. O.T. language
	9. Letters to churches
	11. Inspired by...

What Are The Books Of The Bible?

Activity

- Matchbox Books

Materials

- ❑ Bibles
- ❑ Glue
- ❑ White paper or self-stick mailing labels
- ❑ Scissors

- ❑ Match boxes, large and small
- ❑ Rulers
- ❑ Fine tipped permanent markers
- ❑ Adhesive backed paper (black or any color)

Advance Preparation

- ❑ Collect matchboxes—large and small. Put announcements in church bulletins and newsletters and invite the congregation to save them! 66 small matchboxes are needed per project! [Note: To reduce the number of boxes necessary for the project, do the Old Testament in one session, and the New Testament at another time. Or, create a volume for each major division of the Hebrew Scripture and the Christian Scripture instead of for each specific book. As an alternative, have each student construct one or two books as part of a set for the classroom.]
- ❑ Cut adhesive backed paper to fit the matchboxes.

Method

Select a Bible and turn to the "Table of Contents." Although the Bible can be called "one" book, when we look inside we discover that the Bible is actually 66 separate books. In fact, the word Bible comes from a Greek word meaning "little books."

In order to study Scripture stories it is helpful to know the books of the Bible in order! Review the books of the Old Testament and the New Testament—in sequence—and use this activity to create a mini-library!

Select a small kitchen matchbox for each book of the Bible—66 of them! Cover two sides and the "spine" of each box with adhesive backed paper to form a book jacket. To create the pages, cut a narrow strip of white paper and glue it around the remaining portion of each box. A sticky backed mailing label could be used instead of paper and glue. Draw lines on the white paper to represent pages. Write the name of the book on the spine of each volume. Sequence the mini-books by standing them side by side in order.

As a handy way to keep the individual volumes together, cover several large kitchen matchboxes with adhesive backed paper. Stand the smaller boxes inside of the larger ones and place them end-to-end.

Why Is The Bible Important?

Activity

- Spatter Painted Bookmark

Materials

❏	Bibles	❏	"Fill in the blank" sheet
❏	Duplicating equipment	❏	Paper
❏	Red construction paper	❏	Scissors
❏	Thin tempera paint	❏	Newspapers
❏	15" x 15" pieces of screen	❏	Duct tape
❏	Clean-up supplies	❏	L, O, V, E letter patterns or stencils
		❏	Toothbrushes or vegetable brushes

Advance Preparation

❏ Duplicate a copy of the "Fill in the blank" sheet for each participant.

❏ Prepare several sets of L, O, V, E letter patterns.

❏ Cut sheets of construction paper into quarters or into heart shapes. (Be sure the L O V E letters fit vertically within the size of the bookmark.)

❏ Cover screen edges with duct tape to avoid sharp surfaces.

Method

It is estimated that the 39 books of the Old Testament have 929 chapters, 23,214 verses, and 593,493 words and that the 27 books of the New Testament have 260 chapters, 7959 verses, and 181,253 words. And yet, the central theme of God's Word could be summed up in four letters! Can you guess what they are? Try this activity to find out!

Read the Scripture passages provided and choose one word to complete each sentence. The word will have the same number of letters as the blanks in the sentence. Then, combine the first letter of each word in the blank to form one word that sums up the message of the whole Bible.

Fill In The Blanks!

During Advent we remember stories about the _ _ _ _ _ of Old Testament people. (Deuteronomy 6:7)

At Christmas and Epiphany we celebrate because God gave His _ _ _ _ Son to be our Savior. (John 3:16)

Throughout Lent and Easter we rejoice because Jesus is the _ _ _ _ _ _ over sin and death. (1 Corinthians 15:57)

During Pentecost we remember that the message of the Bible is for _ _ _ _ _ _ _ _. (Matthew 28:19,20)

The message of the Bible is _ _ _ _!

The Bible is important because it tells us how much God loves us and because it teaches us how to show our love for God in return. Make a spatter-painted bookmark to help remember this important message.

Cover the table with newspaper. Choose a piece of red construction paper and set it on the work space. Position the four letters - L O V E - vertically on the bookmark. It may be necessary to place a small piece of tape under each letter to keep it in place. Hold a piece of screen several inches above the paper. Dip a toothbrush or vegetable brush into thin paint and stroke it across the screen to create a spatter-paint effect on the paper. Set aside the screen and carefully remove the letters. An outline of the word "LOVE" will remain.

Answers: LIVES, ONLY, VICTOR, EVERYONE, LOVE

[2]Wilmington, H.L. Wilmington's Book of Lists. Wheaton, IL: Tyndale, 1987.

The Old Testament

God's Word, the Bible, is revealed to us in two testaments—the Old and the New. Testament means covenant, a solemn agreement concerning the relationship of God and God's people—what each will do. According to the Old Testament, the people may expect God's steadfast love and righteous judgment; God may expect faithful devotion and service. The New Testament calls for a new covenant in which God's people respond to God's gift of salvation in Christ with a "new" life.

The Old Testament contains 39 books which are organized into four major categories: Law, History, Poetry, and Prophets. This collection of religious books was written in Hebrew (except for Ezra 4:8-6:18; 7:12-16; and Daniel 2:4b-7:28 which were written in Aramaic, a language closely related to Hebrew) during a period of over 1000 years. It contains stories and psalms, laws and proverbs, history and legend, prophetic proclamations and love songs. The writers were inspired by the Holy Spirit to communicate God's revelations to them and they interpreted God's revelations according to their understanding of God's message of salvation.

In general, the Old Testament illumines the past and present and offers glimpses into the future. Although there are many separate books in this portion of Scripture, each with its own unique message, there is one unifying theme. The Old Testament records God's words, deeds and dealings with humankind during the years before Christ's birth and reveals God's purpose—that all might be saved from sin and live joyfully with God. This remarkable unity can only be attributed to the fact that behind the many human voices of the Bible there is the authority of only one Voice—God's.

Five activities offer an opportunity to review the books of the Old Testament and to learn more about its four major sections—Law, History, Poetry, and Prophets.

Old Testament Review

Activity

- Spinner Game

Materials

- ❏ Heavy paper plates
- ❏ Pencils
- ❏ Markers
- ❏ Tape
- ❏ 8 1/2" x 11" paper
- ❏ "Old Testament Books Of The Bible" sheet
- ❏ Rulers (optional)
- ❏ Scissors
- ❏ Metal paper fasteners
- ❏ Bibles
- ❏ Duplicating equipment
- ❏ Posterboard or cardboard scraps

Advance Preparation

- ❏ Duplicate an "Old Testament Books Of The Bible" sheet for each participant.

Method

One of the first steps in memorizing the 39 books of the Old Testament is becoming familiar with their names. Look up the "Table of Contents" page at the beginning of a Bible. Review the names of the books and the categories into which they are organized. As a way to help learn this information, make a spinner game and play it alone or with another person.

To make the wheel, select a heavy paper plate. Use a pencil to divide the bottom of the plate into four quarters. With markers, color in the sections so that each one is a different shade. Then, print a category—LAW, HISTORY, POETRY, PROPHETS—in each section. Cut a pointed 4" spinner out of posterboard or cardboard. With a scissor point, poke a hole in the wide end of the spinner and in the center of the paper plate. Loosely attach the spinner to the plate with a metal paper fastener and tape the spread prongs in place to the undecorated side of the plate.

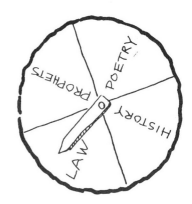

To record responses while playing the game, make an "Old Testament Books of the Bible" sheet or use the copy provided. To make the response form, take a piece of 8 1/2" x 11" paper and fold it into four quarters. Open the sheet and print one of the categories of Old Testament books in each section—LAW, HISTORY, POETRY, PROPHETS. Draw five lines under the word "Law," twelve lines under "History," five lines under "Poetry," and seventeen lines under "Prophets."

To play the game, spin the pointer. When the spinner stops, name one Old Testament book that fits the category where the arrow points. It's ok to use a Bible to help remember the names of the books! To record responses, list the answers on the "Old Testament Books Of The Bible" sheet. Once the page is completed, review the list and memorize the names of the books.

"OLD TESTAMENT BOOKS OF THE BIBLE"

LAW

_____

_____

_____

_____

_____

HISTORY

_____

_____

_____

_____

_____

_____

_____

_____

_____

_____

_____

_____

POETRY

_____

_____

_____

_____

_____

PROPHETS

_____

_____

_____

_____

_____

_____

_____

_____

_____

_____

_____

_____

_____

_____

_____

_____

Law

Activity

- Scroll

Materials

- ☐ Scissors
- ☐ Markers
- ☐ Plain paper or adding machine tape rolls
- ☐ Double-sided tape or glue
- ☐ Markers
- ☐ Ribbon
- ☐ Dowel rods (or chop sticks or pencils)

Method

The first five books of the Bible—Genesis, Exodus, Leviticus, Numbers and Deuteronomy—are commonly called the Law. They are also known by the names Pentateuch, meaning five volumes, Torah or "teachings," and books of Moses. The first book deals with the beginnings of all things and the other four focus on the beginnings of Israel, the nation through which salvation by grace would be available to the entire world.

At one time the books of the Bible were written on scrolls—pieces of paper attached to rods on each side that were rolled up and held together with a fastener. In Hebrew synagogues today the books of the Law are still read from scrolls. Make a scroll as a way to record and review the names of the Old Testament books of the Law.

Cut a piece of plain paper into a long, narrow strip—3" wide x 6" - 8" long—or cut several inches off of a roll of adding machine paper. Using double-sided tape or glue, attach a dowel rod to one end of the paper. Roll the paper around the rod and be sure it is attached securely. Affix a second rod to the other side of the paper. Print the names of the first five books of the Bible on the paper. Roll up the scroll so that the two rods meet in the center. Tie a ribbon around the scroll.

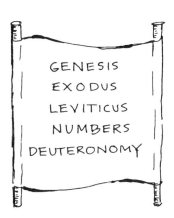

History

Activity

● Game

Materials

❑ Bibles
❑ A answer key
❑ Duplicating equipment

❑ Game sheets
❑ Paper
❑ Buttons or markers

Advance Preparation

❑ To make up new questions, prepare "Tic-Tac-Toe" game sheets. Divide an 8 1/2" x 11" piece of paper into nine sections.

Number each section 1-9 and print or type information about the books of History in each square.

❑ To use the questions provided, duplicate a copy of the "Tic-Tac-Toe" game sheet for each participant.

"TIC-TAC-TOE GAME"

1. Which book contains the story of a woman who choose to serve the God of Israel?	2. Which two books contain the history of the Israelites from Adam through the Babylonian exile?	3. Which book records the story of the conquest of Canaan?
4. Which two books record the life story of David?	5. Which book is the story of a brave woman who saved the Israelites from destruction?	6. Which book tells the story of the rebuilding of Jerusalem?
7. Which two books describe the decline and fall of both Israel and Judah?	8. Which book records the Israelite's ups and downs under the rule of fifteen tribal chiefs?	9. Which book tells the story of the return of the exiles from Babylon to Judea?

● Prepare "Tic-Tac-Toe" Answer Key

"TIC-TAC-TOE ANSWERS"

1. Ruth
2. 1 & 2 Chronicles
3. Joshua
4. 1 & 2 Samuel
5. Esther
6. Nehemiah
7. 1 & 2 Kings
8. Judges
9. Ezra

Method

The twelve books of History—Joshua, Judges, Ruth, 1 and 2 Samuel, 1 and 2 Kings, 1 and 2 Chronicles, Ezra, Nehemiah and Esther—describe the birth of a new Israelite nation. Although each book has its own emphasis, the major theme of this section of Scripture is the blessings of obedience to God and the tragic results of sin.

Play a game of "Tic-Tac-Toe" to learn more about the books of History. Although the game can be played alone by alternating "X" and "O" answers, it would be more fun to find a partner. It's also helpful if a third person or the leader is the "answer checker." One player will be "X" and the other "O."

Determine which person goes first. An easy way to decide is to let the person with the next birthday start. That person reads a question in one of the nine squares and answers it by naming one of the Old Testament books of History. Note that 1 and 2 Samuel, 1 and 2 Kings, and 1 and 2 Chronicles are grouped together so that questions about the twelve books of History fit into the nine squares of the game board! If the answer is correct, the player places his or her marker on the square. In order to re-use the game boards, use buttons or small pieces of paper to cover the squares rather than marking "X" or "O" directly on the sheets.

Now, the other player takes a turn. The first person who places three markers in a row—horizontally, vertically or diagonally—wins the game.

Take home a "Tic-Tac-Toe" sheet and play the game with family and friends as a way to review the books of History.

Poetry

Activity

- Acrostic Poem

Materials

- ❑ Bibles
- ❑ Markers
- ❑ Construction paper
- ❑ Pens

Method

Five diverse books of the Old Testament—Job, Psalms, Proverbs, Ecclesiastes, and Song of Solomon—are known as the books of Poetry, sometimes called the books of Wisdom.

In addition to containing vivid imagery and lofty thought, most poetry today includes orderly rhythm and rhyme. Hebrew poetry is more like free verse, lacking regular meter and rhyme. The book of Job is a dramatic poem that deals with the problem of human suffering. Psalms includes 150 songs of prayer and praise, many of which are quoted in the New Testament and foretell the coming of the Savior. Proverbs provides short statements about successful living. Ecclesiastes contains a debate about the meaning of life. Song of Solomon, or Song of Songs, speaks of God's love for Israel and the relationship of Christ and the church.

Since these books of the Old Testament are known as Poetry, write an Acrostic poem to describe each text. Select a piece of construction paper and print the letters of the word "POETRY" vertically down the left side of the page. Leave space between each letter to write a line about the books of Poetry of the Old Testament. For example:

P oetic books in the Old Testament help us

O bserve suffering in the book of Job;

E xplore prayer and praise in 150 Psalms;

T each tips for successful living in Proverbs;

R espond to the meaning of life in Ecclesiastes;

Y earn for a loving relationship like Christ and the

church in Song of Solomon.

Write several poems, as each one will turn out differently. Leave the Acrostics in the Learning Center for others to read. Remember to take them home at the end of class.

Prophets

Activity

- Magnetic Sequencing Game

Materials

- ❏ 3" x 5" index cards
- ❏ Markers
- ❏ Envelopes
- ❏ Bibles
- ❏ Scissors
- ❏ Magnetic strips
- ❏ Cookie sheet or metal tray

Method

Although they may be called "Major" and "Minor," the seventeen books that form the last section of the Old Testament are all categorized by the word "Prophets." Major and Minor refer to the length of the books—long or short—not to their importance. The five major books of the Prophets include Isaiah, Jeremiah, Lamentations, Ezekiel, and Daniel. Note that Lamentations is actually a poetic book, probably written by Jeremiah. It is not the name of a prophet—a person—like the other books. Minor prophets include Hosea, Joel, Amos, Obadiah, Jonah, Micah, Nahum, Habakkuk, Zephaniah, Haggai, Zechariah, and Malachi.

The prophets were people God used to give messages to His people. The period of the prophets, actually beginning with Samuel, covered about 500 years of Old Testament history. Then for the next 400 years there were no prophets until the coming of John the Baptist in New Testament times. Three words—sin, judgment, and hope summarize the message of the prophets. God sent these messengers to tell people to turn from their sin and to warn them of the consequences. Prophets also told of future events. They said that God would send the Messiah to save His people and that some day the Messiah, Jesus Christ, would rule over the whole world.

Try a magnetic sequencing game as an aid to memorizing the names of these seventeen books of the Prophets. Mark and cut strips from index cards, approximately five inches by one inch. Write or print the name of each book on a separate piece. Cut a section of magnet long enough to support each "Prophet" strip. To use as a teaching tool, scramble the pieces on a metal tray, then try to put them back in the proper sequence.

Label an envelope with the word "Prophets" and store the strips in it. Use the game pieces at home on a tray, metal cabinet, or refrigerator.

The New Testament

What is the New Testament? It's the collection of sacred books that forms the second part of the Bible—God's Word. It's also a promise fulfilled. The New Testament records how the promise God made in the Old Testament—a Messiah to save God's people from their sins—came true through the life, death and resurrection of Jesus. The New Testament also shares what God's promise can mean to everyone who claims it as their own: eternal life.

The New Testament contains 27 books which are organized into four major categories: Gospels, History (Acts), Epistles (Pauline and General) and Prophecy (Revelation or Visions). The New Testament was written in Greek, not "classical" Greek but "common" Greek, the language of everyday life in that time. This collection of religious books was written during a period of about 100 years, in the second half of the first century, within the lifetime of those who were contemporaries of Jesus. Although Jesus left behind no written record of his mission, his apostles—and their disciples—did. Gospels, History, Epistles and Prophecy were written by people whose lives had been transformed by the life of Jesus, whose faith was based on a living Lord, and who were empowered by the Holy Spirit to spread this message.

People who met together for worship continued to read the Old Testament Scriptures and people who knew Jesus—who were "eyewitnesses" to his ministry —were asked to share his teachings. It is believed, and actually documented by early manuscripts, that the first writings were the letters, or epistles, of Paul to the early churches. As time passed and eyewitnesses gradually died, the Christians realized that clear accounts of Jesus' life and work must be written down. Mark, working with Simon Peter, wrote the first Gospel. An additional three Gospels, plus Acts, Revelation, and the General Epistles followed. Once again, the writers were inspired by the Holy Spirit to communicate God's revelations to them, and they interpreted God's revelations according to their understanding of God's message of salvation. Although the twenty-seven books that form the New Testament were agreed upon and widely used by early gatherings of believers, they were formally accepted by the Church Councils of Laodicea (AD 363) and Carthage (AD 397) as the inspired Word of God. While the twenty-seven books were written by a diverse group of people in various times and places, they have two things in common: they teach what the eyewitnesses—particularly the disciples of Jesus—taught, and they encourage and strengthen Christians in their faith.

Five activities offer an opportunity to review the books of the New Testament and to learn more about its four major sections—Gospels, History, Epistles and Prophecy. May all who participate in these projects come to understand the most important message ever given to the world—the message of salvation and hope brought to us through Jesus Christ. And, as Jesus' teachings are applied to life, may each participant grow in faith and further Christ's mission in the world today.

New Testament Review

Activity

- "Go Fish" Game

Materials

- ❑ Markers
- ❑ 3" x 5" index cards
- ❑ Bibles

Advance Preparation

- ❑ Prepare one or more decks of cards to use in the activity.

Method

"Go Fish" is a card game that can be used to teach various topics, including the names of the books of the New Testament. Use the deck of cards provided or make a deck to keep and play the game with another person.

To prepare a set of cards, count out fifty-four 3" x 5" index cards. Letter the name of each New Testament book on two cards. Besides the name of the book, print its category—such as Gospel, History, Epistle or Prophecy. When the deck is completed, find another pupil or leader and play the game.

Mix up the cards. Deal each player five cards. Place the remaining cards in a stack, face down, in the center of the playing space. To begin the game, one player asks another

for the name of a Bible book to match one he or she has in hand. If the player asked has the card, it must be given to the person requesting it. A "pair" is made and the cards are placed on the table. Player One may ask for another card, and may keep asking until the requested card cannot be produced. When that happens, the player must "Go Fish" by drawing a card from the stack on the table. If a match is made from the "Go Fish" pile, that player continues. If not, it is the next person's turn. When all of the cards are matched, the player who has the most sets wins.

Once twenty-seven sets are made, work together to sequence—or put in order—the books of the New Testament. Use the Bible as a guide to become familiar with the names of the books and their placement in Scripture.

Leave the deck of cards for others to use or take it home to share with family and friends.

Gospels

Activity

- Tangram

Materials

☐ Bibles	☐ Pencils
☐ Protractor	☐ Scissors
☐ Paper	☐ Rulers
☐ 3" x 5" index cards	

Method

Gospel is a word that means "Good News." The four Gospels—Matthew, Mark, Luke and John—record the good news of the birth, infancy, teaching, death and resurrection of Jesus. The first three Gospels are the most alike; they cover the same events. Matthew, Mark and Luke are called the "Synoptic" Gospels, which means a "seeing together." Since Mark was the first Gospel to be written, it was used as a source for the other two. John, written later, provides a different perspective on who Jesus is, what he said, and what he did. While John portrays Jesus as the Son of God, Matthew depicts Jesus as King, Mark characterizes him as Servant, and Luke identifies him as the Son of man. Although the

four Gospels are written from unique viewpoints, they have one purpose: " But these are written so that you will put your faith in Jesus as the Messiah and the Son of God. If you have faith in him, you will have true life." (John 20:31)

Construct a tangram to remember the message of the Gospels. Take four 3" x 5" index cards and trim one inch from the short end of two cards. Stack the trimmed and untrimmed cards, then cut a point on one end of all four pieces at the same time. A 90 degree angle will work best.

Review the names of the four Gospels: Matthew, Mark, Luke and John. Copy the four names onto the sections of the tangram—one word per section.

Arrange the pieces with the points touching in the center; be sure to place the longer sections with points together and then fit in shorter cards. What shape does this form? This symbol is a reminder of the message of the Gospels: Jesus is the Savior. The Gospels make it clear that Jesus' death on the cross was part of God's plan to save us from our sins.

History

Activity

- Mobile

Materials

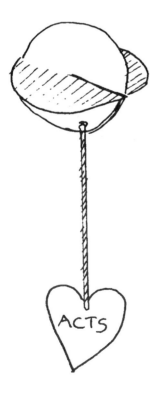

- ❑ Circle pattern
- ❑ Scissors
- ❑ Sponges
- ❑ Thread
- ❑ Paper scraps
- ❑ Bible

- ❑ Pencils
- ❑ Green tempera paint
- ❑ Darning needles
- ❑ Newspaper
- ❑ Pens
- ❑ Blue posterboard or heavy construction paper

Method

Acts, the fifth book of the New Testament, is often called a book of History. Acts records the history of the spread of Christ's Gospel and the growth of the Church. Events in Acts cover about a thirty year period—from Jesus' Ascension in Jerusalem to Paul's preaching in Rome. Written by Luke, Acts emphasizes the power of the Holy Spirit in disseminating Christ's message throughout the world.

Form a mobile to symbolize the theme of Acts: extending the message of salvation from Jerusalem, throughout Palestine, outward to other Mediterranean lands, to Rome, and ultimately throughout the world. Place the circle pattern on the blue paper; then, trace and cut two matching circles. Cut a slit from the outer edge of the circle to the center of both pieces. Lay the circles flat on top of the newspaper-covered work surface. To give the appearance of continents, tap green paint at random around both sides of the blue circles. When the paint is dry, assemble the "world" by interlocking the slit portions of the circles.

Fold a small square of construction paper and cut a cross or a heart shape from it. Unfold the shape, and with a pen, write "ACTS" on both sides of the symbol. Attach the design to the underside of the "world" using the darning needle to sew the thread through the paper. Extend the thread for several inches and then tie the ends to hold the heart in place. Provide a hanging loop for the mobile by following the same procedure with the darning needle and thread.

Hang the mobile where it can swing freely and remember the history lesson from the book of Acts.

Epistles

Activity

- Clothes Pin Game

Materials

- Bibles
- Rulers
- Permanent markers
- Clip clothes pins (22 per person!)
- Posterboard or cardboard
- Scissors or mat knife
- Baskets or boxes

Advance Preparation

- Prepare one game board and 22 game pieces for the Learning Center or cut posterboard or cardboard into one 12" square per participant.

Method

Twenty-one letters, called Epistles, form the majority of the New Testament books. Thirteen letters composed by Paul are known to be the earliest writings in the New Testament. Called the Pauline Epistles, this correspondence is directed to specific churches and individuals. The last eight Epistles are designated as "General" because they are not addressed to specific places or people. Seven of the General Epistles are named for their authors—one each for James and Jude, two for Peter, and three for John. Most scholars consider the authorship of Hebrews to be unknown.

Although each of the letters has its own specific purpose and theme, all twenty-one Epistles amplify and clarify the content of the Gospels, stress the importance of correct doctrine, and relate doctrine to daily life.

Play a game to learn the names and the sequence of the New Testament Epistles. Use the game board and playing pieces provided or make a set to keep. To create a set, cut out or choose a 12" posterboard square. Draw a one inch border around the four sides

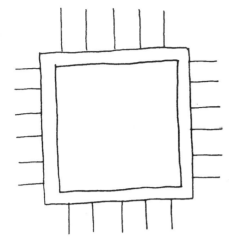

of the square. Divide two sides of the border into six equal sections and the other two sides into five equal sections. Beginning at one corner of the board, letter the word "Epistles" in the first square, print "Pauline" in the next thirteen spaces, and write "General" in the next eight.

To make the playing pieces, count out 22 clip clothes pins. Using permanent marker, print the words "New Testament" on one clothes pin, and letter the name of each Epistle on the remaining twenty-one. [If it is not possible to write directly on the plastic or wood, print the words on small pieces of paper and glue or tape them to the clothes pins.]

Try the game. Mix up the clothes pins, place them in a basket or box, and set the container in the center of the game board. Pick one clothes pin at a time and read the name of the book that's written on it. First, decide if the book is a Pauline Epistle or a General Epistle. Then clip the pin to a square on the board, putting the books in their proper New Testament sequence: Romans, 1 Corinthians, 2 Corinthians, , Ephesians, Philippians, Colossians, 1 Thessalonians, 2 Thessalonians, 1 Timothy, 2 Timothy, Titus, Philemon, Hebrews, James, 1 Peter, 2 Peter, 1 John, 2 John, 3 John, and Jude. The "New Testament" clothes pin should be attached to the square labeled "Epistles." Take the set home and continue to play the game until you can put the Epistles in order without looking in the Bible for help!

Prophecy

Activity

- Diamond Shaped Poem

Materials

- ❑ Construction paper
- ❑ Pens
- ❑ Markers
- ❑ Bible

Method

The Revelation to John can be categorized as a book of Prophecy. The last book of the New Testament is an Apocalypse, a series of inspired visions that reveal a new heaven and a new earth. Although there are many schools of interpretation in regard to Revelation, the book was written to encourage a persecuted Church to endure. God is in control; one day there will be an end to the opposition faced by God's people. Christ came; Christ will come again; God's Kingdom will be supreme.

Summarize the message of Revelation by writing a five line diamond shaped poem. This type of creative writing is a poem in which the lines are opposites, or contrasts, of each other. The formula is:

Line One: One word which is an opposite of line five.
Line Two: Two words which describe line one.
Line Three: Three words which resolve the conflict.
Line Four: Two words which describe line five.
Line Five: One Word which is an opposite of line one.

Select a piece of construction paper and a pen or marker. Follow the formula and write a diamond shaped poem to describe Revelation's message: God is in control of everything—past, present and future! For example:

Good

Triumph of Jesus

Kingdom of God

Defeat of Satan

Evil

Producing The Bible

Pick up a Bible and look through the pages. Have you ever thought of the process of producing the book that you hold in your hands? Actually, the story of the mechanics of making the Bible spans more than 4000 years of world history! Of course, we know that oral traditions of God's love were passed from generation to generation during Bible times, and inspired writing was recorded by Old Testament scribes like Moses, David and Isaiah, and New Testament authors such as Matthew, John, and Paul. But have you ever considered the individuals and groups that invented alphabet systems, writing surfaces, copying processes, and translating techniques? And what about pre-historic ancestors who painted pictures on cave walls, people who invented systems of representing language, Egyptians who made papyrus paper, scribes who copied "jots and tittles," individuals who translated texts, the man who invented a printing press, and countless others! Too often we take all of this for granted!

Five activities offer the opportunity to take time to appreciate the process of producing the Bible! Review the names of the books of the Old and New Testaments and explore some of the mechanics of recording the message of God's love: language systems, writing surfaces, copying processes, and translating techniques. Praise God for the gift of the Bible!

Books Of The Bible Review

Activity

- Paper Chain

Materials

- ❏ Construction paper
- ❏ Pens or markers
- ❏ Staples
- ❏ Bible
- ❏ Scissors
- ❏ Stapler
- ❏ Tape

Advance Preparation

❑ Cut construction paper into 2" x 8" strips.

Method

Create a paper chain as a way to review the names of the books of the Bible and the order in which they are found in the Old and New Testaments. How many strips are needed for a "Books of the Bible" paper chain? Sixty-six!

Cut construction paper into 2" x 8" strips or use the pieces provided. One color or mixed colors will work for the project. Try one color for the books of the Old Testament and another color for the books of the New Testament, or a different color for each category of books such as blue for history, purple for prophets, and red for Gospels.

Find the "Table of Contents" in the front of a Bible. Follow the list and print the name of each book on a separate strip of paper. Stack the strips in sequence, or for an extra challenge, mix up the sixty-six pieces and put them in order without referring to the list.

To create the paper chain, tape or staple the ends of the first strip, "Genesis," together. Slide the second strip, "Exodus," through the first and tape or staple the ends together. Continue adding the strips until all sixty-six have been connected.

Use the paper chain to decorate your room. Review the names of the books and remember that they all contain the same message: God loves you!

Language Systems

Activity

● Code

Materials

❑ Construction paper   ❑ Markers
❑ Pens   ❑ Bible(s)

Method

Did you ever stop to think that language is actually a system of symbols? Each language—German or Greek, Hebrew or Hungarian, has its own "code." Around 30,000 years ago people in pre-historic times painted symbols on cave walls as their language. Through the years stylized pictures developed into alphabets. And, an alphabet is just a symbolic representation of language. Without language, we wouldn't be able to read the Bible! Language helps us learn the Good News of God's love for us! John 3:16 is a familiar verse that reminds us of this important truth. Look up the text in the Bible, read it, and mark the place.

Create your own language—a system of symbols—to communicate the words of John 3:16 to someone else. Select a sheet of construction paper and a marker or pen. On the top of the page write "JOHN 3:16." Next, write the twenty-six letters of the "English" alphabet, making a line under each of them. Create a code—a language—in each of these spaces. For example, you could make a dot under the letter A, an exclamation point under B, a question mark under C, and so forth. Be sure that the "code" for each letter is different. Next, make a small line for each letter in the John 3:16 text. For example, the word "for" would have three lines, "God" would have three lines, and so forth. Now, carefully write your new "code" in the space for each letter of the verse. Once it is finished, trade sheets with another person and try to read the verse in the new language. There should be as many "new" languages as there are people in the class! Thank God for the countless number of people it took to create language systems that help us read God's Word.

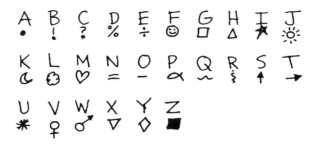

Writing Surfaces

Activity

- Paper Making

Materials

☐ Newspapers ☐ Bucket(s) or washtub
☐ Water ☐ Cornstarch

- ❑ Measuring cups and spoons
- ❑ Rolling pins
- ❑ Paper towels
- ❑ Fine tipped markers or calligraphy pens
- ❑ 6" pieces of screen
- ❑ Plastic wrap
- ❑ Bible(s)
- ❑ Egg beater or wire whisk (or blender or food processor)

Advance Preparation

- Since making homemade paper takes a long time, speed up the process by soaking the newspaper pieces in water for two hours before class begins.

Method

Today the words of the Bible are usually printed on pages made of paper, but it hasn't always been that way. Long ago people carved messages on stone, wrote words on rocks, and painted inscriptions on walls of caves and tombs. Later clay tablets were used as writing surfaces and by 1500 BC writing boards—wood or ivory pieces filled with wax—were invented. Thousands of years ago the Egyptians discovered that they could make paper from the stems of a reed called papyrus that grew around the Nile river. Papyrus stems were cut into thin strips and laid side by side. Another layer was laid cross-wise on top of the first and the layers were pounded to release a glue-like plant sap that held them together. Long strips of papyrus, called scrolls, were used to record the words of the Old Testament. Since papyrus was expensive, ordinary people used broken pieces of pottery, called "sherds," as writing surfaces. Later the skins of sheep and goats were cleaned and treated and made into a type of paper called parchment. In the second century pages of "paper" were fastened together at one side in a system called "codex" to form the first books.

Today handmade paper is a treasured art form. Try a simple method for making a piece of paper and write a special message on it. Follow the directions carefully!

Tear sheets of newspaper into small pieces and fill a bucket or wash-tub half-full. Add enough water to cover the paper. Push all of the pieces into the water so they can soak. Let the mixture stand for two hours. Beat the mixture into a creamy pulp with an egg beater or a wire whisk. Blend until no chunks remain. Dissolve 3 tablespoons of cornstarch in 1 cup of water and add it to the pulp. Mix again. Note that a blender or food

processor can be used to produce the pulp, but be sure to reduce the recipe to fit the size of the appliance.

Submerge a piece of screen in the pulp and pull it out. Repeat this process until the screen has a 1/8" layer of pulp on it. Spread out several sheets of newspaper. Lay the pulp-covered screen on the newspaper. Cover the screen with plastic wrap or layers of paper towels. Use a rolling pin to press out excess water. Set the screen on its side so the air can dry the pulp. When dry, gently peel the recycled paper from the screen.

Although paper is a great invention, the Bible tells us that there's an even better place to record God's word. Look up Psalm 119:11 and neatly letter the words on the homemade paper. Remember to write God's word on your heart, too!

Printing Processes

Activity

- Stamp Printing

Materials

- ❏ Shoe insoles (adhesive backed, if possible)
- ❏ Pens
- ❏ Glue
- ❏ Scrap paper
- ❏ Wooden blocks, metal jar lids or empty film cans
- ❏ Scissors
- ❏ Stamp pads

Method

Printing wasn't invented until the fifteenth century, so before this time all writing had to be hand copied. Special groups of people called Scribes made copies of the Old and New Testaments. Copying Scripture was considered a sacred task, so the scribes checked their work carefully against their source. Sometimes they would count the number of lines and compare them with the original; other times a second scribe would check the whole copy. Later, groups of scribes wrote as the chief scribe read a manuscript aloud.

In the fifth century, hand cut wooden blocks for printing were developed in Asia, and in the early 1400's Johann Gutenberg of Mainz, Germany invented the printing press. The first complete book known to be printed in the Western world was the Bible in 1456.

To remember that printing is an important part of the process of making a Bible, create your own "Printing Press." Use shoe insoles to create stamps. Insoles are made from a thin layer of foam with a layer of latex on top. Some insoles have adhesive backing on one side. Decide on a design to use for the project. It could be a word—such as "BIBLE"—or a symbol like a heart. Draw the outline on the latex side of the insole and cut it out with a scissors. Attach the adhesive backing to a wooden block, a metal jar lid, or an empty film can, or glue the foam in place. Press the printer onto an inked stamp pad and

try the design on paper. A heart symbol would make a great border for the homemade paper made in the "Writing Surfaces" learning center.

Translating Techniques

Activity

- Matching Game

Materials

- ❑ Markers
- ❑ Yarn, string or shoelaces
- ❑ Corrugated cardboard squares, 8 1/2" x 11"
- ❑ Push pins, twenty per project
- ❑ "LOVE LIST"

Advance Preparation

- ❑ Duplicate copies of the "LOVE LIST" or write it on posterboard, newsprint or chalkboard.

LOVE LIST

Czech	Laska
Danish	Elskov
Dutch	Liefde
French	Amour
German	Liebe
Greek	Agape
Italian	Amore
Polish	Milosc
Spanish	Amor
Swedish	Karlek

Method

Since the Old Testament books of the Bible were written in the Hebrew language, with a small portion in Aramaic, and the New Testament Scriptures were written in Greek, the Bibles that are in use today are the result of many translations over hundreds of years. Two early versions were called the Septuagint, a translation from Hebrew to Greek, and the Vulgate, Jerome's translation of the Hebrew and Greek into Latin around 400 A.D. The first translation of the whole Bible into English was made by John Wycliffe in 1384. Today, the Bible is available in more than a thousand languages and translation work to supply God's Word in dialects spoken by small groups of people around the world continues.

Regardless of the language, the message of the Bible can be summed up in one word: LOVE. Learn to write the word "LOVE" in different languages and create a game to help translate this important message.

Choose a cardboard square, a "LOVE LIST," and one or more markers. On the left side of the cardboard, underneath each other, list the names of the countries. Place a push pin at the end of each line. On the right side of the square, in random order, list the word "LOVE" in different languages. At the beginning of each line, place a push pin. Now, try to match the country and the correct translation. Using string, yarn, or shoelaces, attach a piece, approximately 10" - 20" long, to each push pin on the left side of the game board. Beginning with the first country, connect the piece of string to the push pin next to the word "LOVE" written in that language. Continue this procedure until all matches have been made.

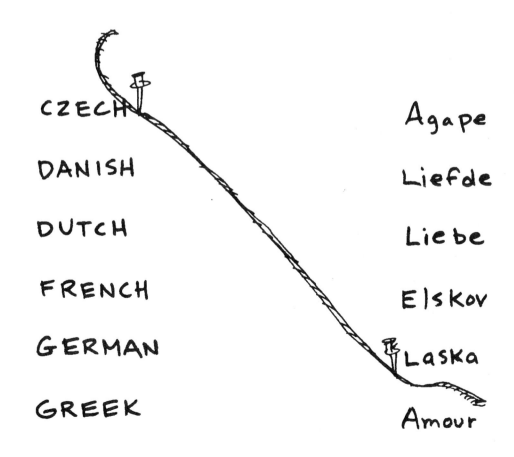

When the activity is completed, unwind the string and invite a family member or friend to try the exercise.

Using The Bible

In previous chapters of <u>Bible Basics</u> topics like "What is the Bible," "The Old Testament," "The New Testament," and "Producing the Bible" are considered. Now it's time to think about "Using the Bible." We need to know how to use the Bible in order to study the Bible. That's basic!

Five activities are designed to help participants consider versions and translations, learn names and abbreviations, develop skills in finding books, chapters and verses, practice cross referencing, and discover additional helps found in many editions of the Bible.

Learning ways to "use" the Bible not only offers participants the occasion to read and study Scripture with new understanding, it also provides them with the opportunity to apply God's Word to their lives.

Versions Of The Bible

Activity

- Board Game

Materials

- Bibles, various versions
- Markers
- Index cards
- Buttons (one per player)
- Posterboard
- Rulers or yardsticks
- Pens
- Spinner (from another game or made with cardboard and a paper fastener)

Advance Preparation

- Prepare the game board as illustrated. Write a different direction in each square, such as Yellow, Blue, Go back 1, Move ahead 2, Skip a turn, Spin again.

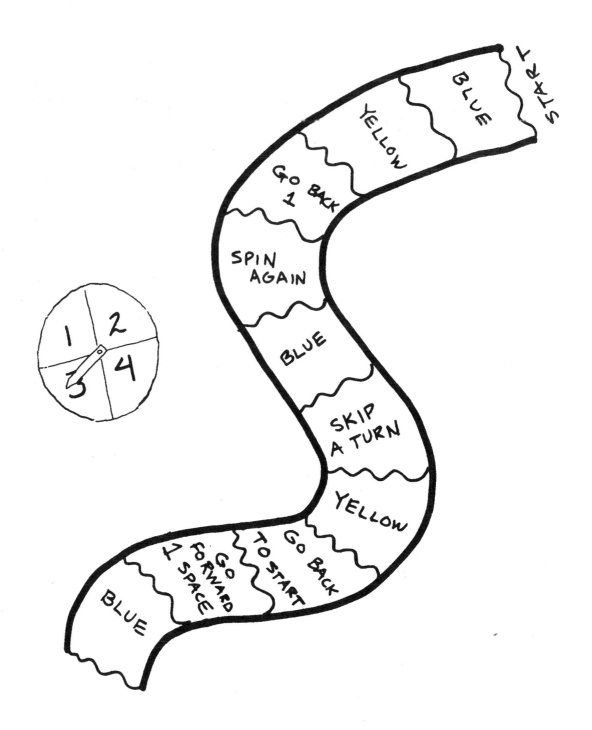

❑ Write questions and information on two different colors of index cards, for example:

YELLOW CARDS

1. The Old Testament was originally written in the _____ language.

2. The New Testament was originally written in the _____ language.

3. Biblical scholars use ancient _____ to help them translate God's Word from the original languages.

4. King _____ of England authorized a version of the Bible in 1611.

5. The letters NRSV stand for the _____ version of the Bible.

6. New translations of God's Word help to make the Bible easier to _____.

7. Although it is good for devotional reading, a _____ is not as true to the original text as other versions and translations.

8. The invention in the middle of the fifteenth century that revolutionized the spread of ideas was _____.

9. The Contemporary English Version, also known as the _____, is a good choice for beginning Bible readers, children and youth.

10. As we read any version of the Bible, the _____ helps us apply God's Word to our lives.

ANSWERS

1. Hebrew; 2. Greek; 3. Manuscripts; 4. James; 5. New Revised Standard Version; 6. Read or understand; 7. Paraphrase; 8. Printing; 9. CEV; 10. Holy Spirit

BLUE CARDS

1. The King James Version (KJV) is the translation authorized by King James of England in 1611.

2. The New Revised Standard Version (NRSV) of 1989 was updated from the Revised Standard Version (RSV) of 1952. It is a careful and accurate translation by a group of 30 respected scholars.

3. New International Version (NIV), 1978, is a more recent translation than the KJV. Its language is contemporary and easier to understand.

4. The Vulgate, 400 AD, was the first official translation of the Bible into Latin.

5. In 1382 John Wycliffe translated the Vulgate into English.

6. The Septuagint is the name of the first translation from Hebrew to Greek.

7. The Living Bible is a paraphrase rather than a word-for-word translation and is a good version for devotional reading.

8. The Good News Bible, also called Today's English Version, is based on spoken rather than written language.

9. Two Bibles commonly used in the Roman Catholic church are the Jerusalem Bible and the New American Bible.

10. Translation work continues so people throughout the world can read God's word in their own languages.

Method

What version, or translation, of the Bible are you using? Open the book to the title page. It will usually read "The Holy Bible" and list the version, for example "Contemporary English Version" or "New Revised Standard Version." Although the Old Testament was originally written in Hebrew—with a small portion in Aramaic—and the New Testament in Greek, translations, revisions and paraphrases of God's Word have been made so that people can read the Good News in languages they understand.

Translations of the Bible are made from ancient manuscripts. Few Old Testament manuscripts exist, and those that do are in poor shape. Some are only a few inches—or less—square. More New Testament manuscripts are available. Biblical scholars study the ancient manuscripts, and more as they are found, and continue to improve the translations. New translations also reflect archeological finds and changes in the language spoken by the reader.

To learn more about some of the important translations of the Bible, use the board provided and play a game. Although the game may be played alone, it might be more fun to share the experience with at least one more person.

To begin the game, shuffle the blue cards and the yellow cards separately and place each stack on the game board. Each player places a button on the square labeled "Start." One person twirls the spinner and moves to the appropriate square. The person follows the directions written on that square, for example—Spin Again, Lose a Turn, and so forth. If the player lands on a "Yellow" square, the person picks a yellow card, reads the question and tries to answer it. If the correct answer is given, he or she stays on that square. If an incorrect answer is given, the player must return the marker to the square it was on at the beginning of that turn. If the player lands on a "Blue" square, the person picks a blue card and reads the information about "Versions of the Bible" to the rest of the players. He or she stays on that square. Continue until one player reaches the finish line.

Book Names And Abbreviations

Activity

- Lotto Game

Materials

- [ ] Posterboard
- [ ] Markers
- [ ] Index cards
- [ ] Yardstick
- [ ] Bibles

Method

In any book, including the Bible, the Table of Contents lists the arrangement of the subject matter. In a Bible, the table of contents lists the books of the Old and New Testaments in sequence and provides page numbers to help the reader locate them.

Usually the name of each book is "spelled out" in the table of contents, but often it is abbreviated in other places. It's important to know both ways of locating a book. Use a game of Bible lotto to match the "full" name of a book with its shortened version.

To make a game board, divide a piece of posterboard into sixty-six equal sections, for example eleven rows of six. Letter the name of each book of the Bible, in sequence, in a separate square. Place the game board on a flat surface, like a table or desk. Using index cards, print the abbreviation for each book on a separate card.

Old Testament:

Genesis	Gen
Exodus	Ex
Leviticus	Lev
Numbers	Num
Deuteronomy	Deut
Joshua	Josh
Judges	Judg
Ruth	Ruth
1 Samuel	1 Sam
2 Samuel	2 Sam
1 Kings	1 Kings
2 Kings	2 Kings
1 Chronicles	1 Chron (1 Chr)
2 Chronicles	2 Chron (2 Chr)
Ezra	Ezra
Nehemiah	Neh
Esther	Esth
Job	Job
Psalms	Ps
Proverbs	Prov
Ecclesiastes	Eccl
Song of Solomon	Song
Isaiah	Isa
Jeremiah	Jer
Lamentations	Lam
Ezekiel	Ezek
Daniel	Dan
Hosea	Hos
Joel	Joel
Amos	Am
Obadiah	Ob
Jonah	Jon

Micah	Mic
Nahum	Nah
Habakkak	Hab
Zephaniah	Zeph
Haggai	Hag
Zechariah	Zech
Malachi	Mal

New Testament:

Matthew	Mt
Mark	Mk
Luke	Lk
John	Jn
Acts of the Apostles	Acts
Romans	Rom
1 Corinthians	1 Cor
2 Corinthians	2 Cor
Galatians	Gal
Ephesians	Eph
Philippians	Phil
Colossians	Col
1 Thessalonians	1 Thess
2 Thessalonians	2 Thess
1 Timothy	1 Tim
2 Timothy	2 Tim
Titus	Titus
Philemon	Philem
Hebrews	Heb
James	Jas
1 Peter	1 Pet
2 Peter	2 Pet
1 John	1 Jn
2 John	2 Jn
3 John	3 Jn
Jude	Jude
Revelation	Rev

To play the game, shuffle the cards and stack them in a pile. Participants take turns drawing a card and matching the abbreviation to the name of the book on the board. If a match is made, the card should be placed in the proper section on the board. Use Bibles to check answers. Depending on time, instruct each player to make five or ten matches, or to play the entire game.

Book, Chapter, And Verse

Activity

- Punctuation Pin

Materials

- Bibles
- Safety pins
- Newsprint, Posterboard or chalkboard
- Masking tape or glue
- Chalk or markers
- Permanent markers
- Plastic lids (from chip and syrup cans)

Advance Preparation

- Write the punctuation marks . , - : on newsprint, posterboard or a chalkboard.

Method

. , : - At first glance, this series of marks might look like a typing error. Upon closer inspection, however, the "list" contains commonly used methods of punctuation. For purposes of this activity the symbols will serve as tools that help locate books, chapters, and verses in the Bible.

Think about the purpose of each of the four punctuation marks. A period is used at the end of a sentence; it means "stop." A comma indicates a slight separation of sentence elements. A colon comes before a long quotation, explanation, example, or series, or after the salutation of a formal letter. A hyphen is used between the parts of a compound word or the syllables of a divided word. These four punctuation marks are commonly used in Scripture citations, often called Scripture references. In order to know how to find Bible books, chapters and verses, it is important to know what the symbols mean in this context.

In a Scripture reference, the name of the book is listed first. For example, to find the verse called the "Gospel in a nutshell," the Scripture reference would begin by listing the book, "John." In order to locate the correct place in the book of John, the chapter number would come next, "3." The next number(s) indicate the verse(s) to be read. A period (.) or a colon (:) appears between the chapter number and the verse numbers. If a hyphen (-) appears between the numbers it means read ALL verses from the first number to and including the last number. If a comma (,) appears between the numbers it means read ONLY the verses of the numbers listed. So the Scripture reference John 3:16 would tell you to read the sixteenth verse of the third chapter of the book of John. If the citation was John 3:16, 17, it would tell you to read verses sixteen and seventeen, and if it was John 3:16-18, it would indicate that you should start reading at verse sixteen and continue through verse eighteen.

As a unique way to explain this system to someone else, make pins or buttons containing the four punctuation marks. Select a plastic lid to use for the project. Any size or color is fine! Using permanent marker, write the four punctuation marks on the lid. Tape or glue a safety pin to the back of the badge. Wear the "Punctuation Pins" and tell others how to find Scripture references in the Bible.

Cross References

Activity

- Cross Bookmark

Materials

- ❑ Paper
- ❑ Posterboard or manila file folders
- ❑ Liquid tempera paint
- ❑ Teaspoons
- ❑ Pattern for cross
- ❑ Pens or pencils
- ❑ Scissors
- ❑ Liquid starch
- ❑ Glue
- ❑ Bibles (various editions with cross-references)
- ❑ Plastic squeeze-bottles with tips (glue bottles or catsup or mustard containers)

Advance Preparation

- ❑ Duplicate the cross-reference questions for each participant or write them for all to see.
- ❑ Pour a different color of paint into each squeeze bottle. Add about 1 teaspoon of liquid starch to each bottle of paint. Tightly screw the lids on the bottles.

Method

Cross references are a reference from one part of a book to another. It's almost like saying, "For further information see ..." Many editions of the Bible make extensive use of cross-reference notes. As they are used in the Bible, cross references help the reader see the relationship of various passages in Scripture to other texts. Many times the references direct us to similar narratives about the same story; other times they suggest passages that provide additional information on the topic.

Different editions of the Bible use different systems of cross referencing. Some place references in a center column, others put them at the bottom of the page, and several print notes in the page margins. Cross references are easy to use when they are placed directly under the bold-print heading in the text.

Try using cross references to locate several passages of Scripture. Select a Bible—maybe more than one edition—and answer a few questions. Look for the cross references in various locations on the pages.

QUESTIONS

1. The Ten Commandments are listed in Exodus 20:2-17 and _____.

2. The Lord's Prayer can be found in Luke 11:2-4 and _____.

3. Three Gospels record the story of Jesus' resurrection. In Matthew it's located in chapter 28 verses 1-10. Where can it be found in Luke and John?

4. Luke 2 records the story of the birth of Jesus. The Old Testament Scripture that prophesied that Jesus would be born in Bethlehem is found in _____.

5. During the crucifixion Jesus said "I am thirsty." This fulfilled the Scripture recorded in _____.

ANSWERS

1. Deuteronomy 5:1-22

2. Matthew 6:9-15

3. Luke 24:1-12; John 20:1-10

4. Micah 5:2

5. Psalm 2:1-3.

Continue the process of looking up cross references as long as time and interest allow. Then pick a set of cross references—for example Matthew 6:9-15 and Luke 11:2-4, the passages containing "The Lord's Prayer" —and turn them into a bookmark.

Using the cross pattern, trace the shape onto a piece of heavy paper and cut it out. Select one or two colors of paint. Write one verse on the horizontal portion of the cross and the other on the vertical section. Tip the bottle against the paper and squeeze gently to obtain the desired amount of paint. Use the tip of the squeeze bottle to form the desired letters and numbers. Draw additional designs to decorate the bookmark.

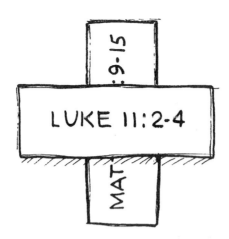

When the paint is dry place the bookmark in your Bible. Remember that cross-references not only help us see the relationship between various passages of Scripture; they also help us remember that all Scripture refers us to the main symbol of God's love—the cross.

Supplements

Activity

- Bible Cover

Materials

❑ Bible	❑ Scissors
❑ Rulers	❑ Pencils
❑ Scrap paper	❑ Fabric paint
❑ Paint brushes	❑ Iron
❑ Waxed paper	❑ Fabric glue
❑ Chalk	❑ Clean up supplies
❑ Sturdy fabric such as denim, canvas, corduroy, twill or drapery fabric	

Advance Preparation

❑ Invite each participant to bring a Bible.

❑ Set up an ironing station and recruit an adult to supervise this portion of the activity.

Method

In the other activities you have used your Bible to discover the version, the abbreviations for the thirty-nine books of the Old Testament and the twenty-seven books of the New Testament, and the cross-referencing system. Look through the pages—from cover to cover—to see what other Bible study aids your Bible provides. It might include:

- Preface or Introduction—Tells what's unique about this particular Bible;

- Time line— A chronology of Bible and world events;

- Notes—Helps for understanding culture, history, context, difficult passages, theological concepts;

- Maps—Key places mentioned in the Bible;

- Charts and diagrams— Aids for visualizing difficult concepts or relationships;

- Pictures—Illustrations of the stories;

- Index—Guide to finding what's where in the book;

- Dictionary or concordance—Additional information about subjects and themes.

All of these study aids, plus additional tools found in various editions, are intended to help the reader understand God's Word and respond to God's teachings.

Make and use a book cover as a reminder of what's contained in your own personal Bible.

Choose fabric that you like; then open your Bible on top of the cloth. In order to measure the correct size, add 1 1/2 inches along the top and bottom edges of the book for a hem allowance. Extend the cloth about four inches beyond both right and left sides of the Bible to form end flaps.

Set aside the Bible until later. Proceed to the ironing area and allow an adult to help with this part of the activity. On the top and bottom edges of the fabric, fold over a "hem" approximately 1 1/2 inches (the finished height of the cloth should be just a tiny bit taller than the height of the Bible). Iron the fabric with firm pressure and warm enough temperature to give a sharp crease along the top and bottom of the material. If the cloth does not hold a crease, use some small dots of fabric glue inside the hem, but do not fasten the four-inch flap allowance on each end of the fabric book cover.

Lay the spine of the open Bible in the center of the creased cloth. Slide the left cover of the Bible into the "pocket" formed by the folded hems; then lift the center of the book enough to slide the right cover into the "pockets" on the other side.

On a piece of scrap paper, plan a design for the cover you have made. Include words or symbols to indicate the contents of the book.

Remove the cover from your Bible. It will be easier to paint if the cover is lying flat on the work surface. Be sure to mark with chalk or pencil where you want the painting to be. Place a piece of waxed paper under the cloth to prevent painted areas from sticking to the work surface.

Use fabric paints in tubes or apply paint with a brush to create the design. Take care to plan and to keep the decoration simple. Too much paint may peel away or may make the Bible hard to handle. Allow the paint to dry according to directions on the tube or bottle. Now you are ready to cover your Bible! When you look at the cover, remember the many ways to use the Bible to read, understand and apply God's word to your life.

Studying The Bible

What's in your tool box? Actually, the answer to that question depends on the type of work you plan to do with the tools, doesn't it? Tools are instruments or implements that serve as a means; things that help to get a job done. So, if you want to build something, your tool box might hold a hammer, nails, saw, and ruler. If you plan to fix something, it might contain pliers, wood glue, screwdrivers and clamps. If you want to go fishing, the tool box would carry bobbers, hooks, lures, and weights. If you want to create a picture, the toolbox should have paints, brushes, pencils and paper. And, if you want to study God's Word, your tool box might contain an atlas, commentary, concordance, and dictionary.

There are many different types of tools to help students of Scripture discover the meaning of the Bible and to help them apply God's Word to their lives. Five activities developed in this session are intended to help you become familiar with some of these resources. Begin by reviewing the names of the books of the Old and New Testaments and continue by exploring the use of an atlas, commentary, concordance, and dictionary. A Bible atlas is a collection of maps showing the lands and the location of events in the Bible. Commentaries, single books or many volumes, are tools to help explain and interpret the Scriptures. Works by many authors with varying viewpoints are available. A Concordance is an alphabetical index of the principal words in the Bible that help relate ideas and doctrines to passages in other books and chapters. A Bible dictionary is an alphabetical listing of Biblical terms and subjects that helps to explain their meanings and applications.

Remember that many other tools for Scripture study are available. They include Bible encyclopedias, books of lists, and handbooks—to name a few. Ask an adult—parent, pastor or teacher—to help you find some of these sources. Being a student of the Bible is a life-long process of filling your tool box with resources that will help you read God's Word in meaningful and memorable ways!

Books Of The Bible Review

Activity

- Two-part Puzzle

Materials

- ❑ Crayons or markers
- ❑ Manila envelopes
- ❑ Scissors
- ❑ Cardboard, cereal or shirt boxes, or 5" x 7" index cards

Method

One helpful tool for studying Scripture is the Table of Contents located in the front of a Bible. It lists the names of the books of the Old and New Testaments in sequence. Although it's handy to have this quick reference guide, it's a great goal to learn how to find the books without having to stop to look up their arrangement each time. One way to learn the names and the organization of the books of the Bible is by making and using simple two part puzzles.

Cut cardboard into 5" x 7" pieces, or use 5" x 7" index cards for the project. Sixty-six rectangles are needed if a puzzle is made for each book of the Bible, however it's possible to do just the Old Testament or New Testament books, or even sections—like History, Prophets, or Writing—within these two categories. Once the pieces are cut, draw a wiggly line down the center of each rectangle.

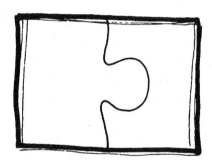

On the left side of each piece, write the number "1" on the first puzzle, "2" on the second puzzle, and so forth until there is a number on each card that corresponds with the number of books you have decided to use for the project.

On the right hand side of each numbered puzzle, write the name of the corresponding book of the Bible. For example, on the "1" puzzle, print "Genesis," on the "2" puzzle write "Exodus," on the "40" puzzle, print "Matthew," and on the "66" puzzle, letter "Revelation."

Last, cut each rectangle apart along the wiggly line to create a two piece puzzle. Mix up the pieces and try putting them together by matching the number with the name. Store the set in a box or manila envelope and share the game with family and friends.

Atlas

Activity

- Atlas Study

Materials

- Bible Atlas(es)
- Paper
- Bible(s)
- Pens

Method

Have you ever used an atlas? An atlas is a book of maps, and a Bible atlas is a book of maps of Bible lands at various periods of history. This tool helps students of the Scripture put information about the people, places and events of the Bible into perspective.

Select a piece of paper to record responses and use an atlas(es) to do the following:

- **A** - Ancient cities: Look up your favorite Old Testament story in the Bible and find the area on a map where it took place.

- **T** - Topography: Locate the city of Jerusalem. Refer to the small symbols or pictures on the map and determine if it is a mountainous or a desert region.

- **L** - Lakes: The Sea of Galilee is the site of many New Testament Bible stories. Locate this body of water on a map. Throughout history The Sea of Galilee has had several other names. Refer to earlier maps and find two different names for this important body of water.

- **A** - Approximate Distance: Find a map of Paul's Missionary journeys. Using the scale on the map, in miles or kilometers, approximate the distance from Jerusalem to Antioch.

- **S** - Study: Locate an ancient and a current map of Israel, often referred to as "The Holy Land." Study the differences and similarities between names and locations then and now.

Commentary

Activity

- Cinquain Poem

Materials

- Bible(s)
- Pens
- Paper
- Commentaries, including one on the Psalms

Method

A Bible commentary is a study tool that helps students understand Scripture and apply its message to their lives. This valuable reference aid "comments" on—or explains—the text. Verse by verse, it interprets words and phrases within the passage and sets the words in the context of the time in which they were written. There are one-volume commentaries on the entire Bible, as well as commentaries with separate volumes for individual books of the Old and New Testaments.

Look up a favorite passage of Scripture, Psalm 23. Read it in one or more versions of the Bible. To gain a better understanding of this text, locate information about Psalm 23 in a commentary. What do some of the phrases mean: "I shall not want," "valley of the shadow of death," and "rod and staff?" Read the commentary, or explanation, to gain a better understanding of David's beautiful words.

Add your own commentary on Psalm 23 by writing a creative interpretation of the passage in the form of a Cinquain poem. Cinquain is a five-line poem that follows this pattern:

Line One -

A one word title that is the subject of the poem

Line Two -

Two words that describe line one

Line Three -

Three action words

Line Four -

Four words that express a feeling about the subject

Line Five -

A synonym (renames or means the same) for line one.

For example:

Shepherd

Caretaker; Guardian

Defends; Preserves; Protects

Loving and caring friend

God

Choose a piece of paper and a pen and write one or more cinquain "commentaries" on Psalm 23.

Concordance

Activity

- Key Mobile

Materials

- Bible(s)
- Construction paper
- Pencils
- Stapler
- Markers
- Tape
- Hole punch
- Key pattern
- Posterboard strips
- Scissors
- Staples
- Thread
- Yarn
- Concordances—concise and exhaustive

Method

Did you ever want to find a verse in the Bible but you just didn't know where to look? The tool for this job is called a concordance. A concordance is a resource that helps people locate a Scripture passage when they only know a key word or a key phrase from the verse. There are separate concordances for each major translation of the Bible, and these are divided into two types—concise and exhaustive. Concise concordances include many of the important words found in the Bible, while exhaustive concordances provide a complete alphabetical listing of all of the words found in the sixty-six books of the Old and New Testaments with references to all of the passages in which they occur.

To use a concordance, look up a key word from the passage you want to find. Following the word will be a list of verses, along with the portion of each passage that includes the key word. It's helpful to remember to look up a word that's important in the verse, but not too common. Otherwise there will be too many references to review!

Choose several key words from your favorite Bible verses and look them up in a concordance. Or try finding words contained in familiar passages: "shepherd" from the famous song of David; "mother," a reference from one of the commandments; "world," a key word in a New Testament summary of the Gospel; and "bread," a term in a petition of the Lord's Prayer. Since knowing how to locate "key" words in the Bible is an important Bible study tool, assemble a simple mobile made of key shapes.

Choose a bright assortment of colored paper. Trace the key pattern and cut out several keys for the mobile. Write a "key" word on one side of each shape and a Scripture reference on the other side. Punch a hole in the top of each key and tie a piece of thread through the opening. Secure with a piece of tape.

Use a marker to write on the posterboard strip: Concordance—Key Words. Staple the posterboard strip into the shape of a circle. Tie or tape the threaded keys to the ring to create the mobile. Adjust the string, so the keys hang at different levels. Punch three holes, equally spaced in the circular strip and attach yarn. Tie the three yarn ends together to make a hanger for the mobile. Hang the colorful mobile where it will catch a breeze and swing around for all to see.

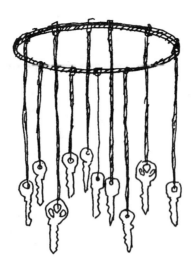

Bible Dictionary

Activity

- Definition Device

Materials

- Children's and Adult Bible Dictionaries
- Rubber bands (two per project)
- Scissors
- Circle pattern (or jar lid or drinking glass)
- Lightweight cardboard or posterboard squares, 5" x 5"
- Markers
- Hole punch
- Bible(s)

Method

Just about everybody has used a dictionary—an alphabetical listing of words that explain their meaning—but have you ever used a Bible dictionary? A Bible Dictionary defines words found in the Old and the New Testaments. It helps students learn to spell and to pronounce the words contained in God's Word. Sometimes it includes pictures or illustrations to help people understand the terms. Bible dictionaries often refer learners to other places in Scripture where the word is located.

Words in a Bible Dictionary are listed in alphabetical order. Guide words on the top of each page help people find a specific word, even if they don't know its exact spelling. Usually, the information includes a pronunciation guide, a simple definition, a detailed, accurate illustration, and additional Scripture references.

Bible dictionaries make learning fun! Try it! Page through Bible dictionaries—child and adult versions—and look up several words. Locate the name of a person, a place, a food, and an animal for starters. Try finding words like Mordecai, Bethlehem, unleavened bread, and adder. Choose one word and its definition and turn it into a "Definition Device" to use to help you review and remember the word and its meaning.

To make a "Definition Device," cut a circle about 3" in diameter from lightweight cardboard or posterboard. Use a jar lid, a drinking glass, or the pattern provided as a template. Punch two holes—one on the right and one on the left side of the circle. Print the word on one side of the circle and letter the definition on the back of the shape, upside-down. Loop a rubber band through each hole and pull to secure.

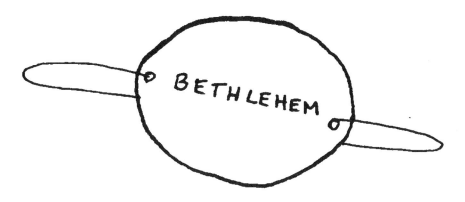

To spin the message, slip your index fingers through the rubber bands and wind tightly. Spread your hands apart to let your message spin into view. As the "Definition Device" spins the message blends together right before your eyes!

Sharing The Bible

Look up Matthew 28:18-20, the passage known as "The Great Commission." In the Contemporary English Version of the Bible, it reads "Jesus came to them and said: I have been given all authority in heaven and on earth! Go to the people of all nations and make them my disciples. Baptize them in the name of the Father, the Son, and the Holy Spirit, and teach them to do everything I have told you. I will be with you always, even until the end of the world." Turn to Acts 1:8. In the CEV it reads "But the Holy Spirit will come upon you and give you power. Then you will tell everyone about me in Jerusalem, in all Judea, in Samaria, and everywhere in the world."

That's Bible Basics! The basic message of the Bible is clear. Everyone who knows the story of God's love is challenged to share it with others. Everyone is called to be a missionary. The word "mission" comes from the Latin word "missio" which means "a sending away." Jesus was sent to the world by the Father for the salvation of those who believe in him. Jesus wants his followers to share that Good News, or Gospel, with the world so that all may hear of his love. Hearing, however, is not enough. People must also experience Jesus' love in order for them to understand the message. Being a missionary involves not only telling about Jesus' love, but also demonstrating that love in action. Missions also requires that people be "called out" of the world to become followers, or disciples, of Jesus. The word which is translated "church" in the New Testament means "those who are called out; those who are sent." People are sent to their neighbors, their friends, and even to people they do not know, to share the story of God's love. Regardless of where people are "sent"—across the street or around the world—all are sent in Jesus' name to share God's love and to invite other people to know and follow Jesus.

Five learning activities in this chapter are designed to help participants explore and experience ways in which they can be missionaries in their present situations.

Dance Directions

Activity

- Macarena

Materials

- ❑ CD or cassette player (optional)
- ❑ Music to the "Macarena"

Method

Share God's love everywhere, every way! Share God's love with everyone, everyday! Share God's love—Jesus showed us the way. Yes! Mission matters! The message of the Bible can be summed up in these words. And, these words can be set to music and demonstrated through movement using the tune of the popular dance fad, the "Macarena."

Modify the motions and add new words to the tune to sing and dance a mission message.

Share God's
[Extend right arm in front of body.]
Love
[Extend left arm in front of body.]
Everywhere
[Turn right arm with palm facing up.]
Every way.
[Turn left arm with palm facing up.]
Share God's
[Bend right arm at elbow and touch left arm at elbow.]
Love
[Bend left arm at elbow and touch right arm at elbow.]
With everyone
[Extend right arm at side.]
Everyday.
[Extend left arm at side.]
Share God's
[Cross right arm over chest.]
Love
[Cross left arm over chest.]
Jesus
[Stretch right arm upward.]
Showed us the way.
[Stretch left arm upward.]
Yes!
[Clap hands overhead or snap fingers.]
Mission matters!
[Improvise action such as clapping, turning, or wiggling.]

Memorized Messages

Activity

- Magnet

Materials

- ❏ Bibles (various translations)
- ❏ Scissors
- ❏ Narrow ribbon or yarn
- ❏ Magnetic strip
- ❏ Glue gun or tacky glue
- ❏ Nutcrackers and nut picks
- ❏ Paper slips
- ❏ Walnuts in the shell
- ❏ Pens or fine-tipped markers

Advance Preparation

- ❏ Cut the magnetic strip into a small piece for each walnut shell.

Method

John 3:16 is one of the most well-known—and well-loved—verses in the Bible. In the CEV it reads "God loved the people of this world so much that he gave his only Son, so that everyone who has faith in him will have eternal life and never really die." Look up John 3:16 in several translations of the Bible.

This verse has been called "The Gospel in a Nutshell." That means that this text shares the basic message of the Bible: God's love. Make a magnet as a reminder of the "Gospel in a nutshell."

Select a walnut and use a nutcracker to open it. Crack it carefully and keep the two halves intact. Use a nut pick to remove the nut meats from the shell. They may be eaten or set aside. Glue about eight inches of ribbon or yarn width-wise to the outside of one of the nut halves. Attach a piece of magnet and set the shell aside so the glue can dry.

Select a favorite translation of John 3:16 and copy the verse onto a paper strip. Roll the strip into a tiny scroll and place it inside the nutshell with the magnet. In addition, learn the verse by heart because it is the heart of the Bible's message.

Fit the two halves together to enclose the scroll, then tie a bow around the "lid" to hold the shells securely. Share the "Gospel In A Nutshell" by giving the magnet to someone else.

Project Possibilities

Activity

- Collage

Materials

- ❏ Materials from "Mission" agencies
- ❏ Bulletin Board
- ❏ Tape
- ❏ Glue
- ❏ Posterboard
- ❏ Tacks
- ❏ Scissors

Advance Preparation

❏ Obtain information on organizations that share God's Word such as:

AMERICAN BIBLE SOCIETY
    1865 Broadway
    New York, NY 10023
    (212) 408-1200

Organization with the mission to provide God's Word in a language people can understand and at a price they can afford.

THE BIBLE LEAGUE
    16801 Van Dam Road
    South Holland, IL 60473
    (708) 331-2094

This organization sponsors a "Children Caring For Children" project which involves purchasing Bibles for young people in other lands.

DENOMINATIONAL MISSION BOARDS
    Various addresses

Many mission boards offer "Bible" projects in which children may be involved.

GIDEONS INTERNATIONAL
    2900 Lebanon Road
    Nashville, TN 37214
    (615) 883-8533

Founded in 1898, the purpose of this group of Christian business and professional lay people is to win people to Christ through the distribution of Testaments and Bibles. The Gideons are active in most countries of the world.

WYCLIFFE BIBLE TRANSLATORS
    P. O. Box 2727
    Huntington Beach, CA 92647
    (714) 969-4600

Committed to the urgent task of translating God's Word into the language of Bible-less people, it is currently working on hundreds of languages in many countries. They are also involved in teaching linguistics, literacy, and translating techniques.

Method

There are many denominational agencies and non-denominational organizations involved in the work of sharing God's Word locally, regionally, nationally, and internationally. Learn more about the important ministries of Scripture distribution and Bible translation that is taking place throughout the world.

Review the information about various groups. Choose one organization and create a collage about its mission. A collage is an art form in which bits of objects are pasted together on a surface. Select a piece of posterboard. Cut pictures and words from materials representing one organization. Arrange the pieces on the paper and glue them in place. Display the collage on a bulletin board. Review collages made by other students to learn about the diversity and direction of mission organizations. Remember that another way to support a mission project is with offerings and prayers.

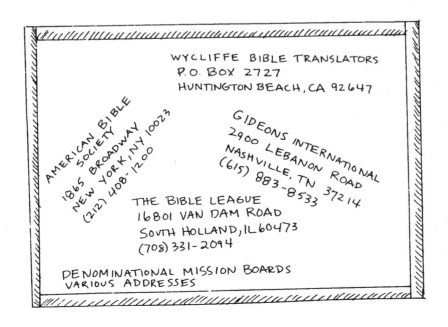

Story Spoons

Activity

- Spoon Puppet

Materials

- ☐ Spoons (plastic or wooden)
- ☐ Tacky glue
- ☐ Fabric scraps
- ☐ Pipe cleaners
- ☐ Permanent markers
- ☐ Yarn or materials for hair
- ☐ Scissors

Method

People who love Jesus are called to be missionaries; to be people who share God's love with others. Make a spoon puppet to represent yourself and use it to tell others what you are doing and what you will do to share God's love.

Select a spoon to use for the project. Using permanent markers, draw a face on the curved side of the spoon. Add hair by gluing yarn, cotton or felt to the top of the spoon. Twist a pipe cleaner around the neck of the puppet to form arms. Make a simple costume by cutting a rectangle or triangle of fabric the length of the distance from the neck to the bottom of the spoon. Cut a small slit one-quarter inch from the top of the costume and slide the spoon through it. Glue the costume in place on both sides of the neck. Add trims.

Form groups of two or four and take turns using the puppets to introduce each other and to present at least one idea for sharing God's love with others.

T-Shirt Themes

Activity

- T-shirt

Materials

- ❑ T-shirts
- ❑ Paper
- ❑ Iron
- ❑ Brown paper
- ❑ Fabric crayons
- ❑ Pencils
- ❑ Ironing board
- ❑ Bibles

Advance Preparation

- ❑ Invite each participant to bring a T-shirt for the project.
- ❑ Recruit extra adults to supervise the ironing station.
- ❑ Set up the ironing board and pre-heat the iron to a very high setting.

Method

Jesus entrusted the disciples with the task of spreading the message of God's love. He told them to preach and teach and baptize in his name. This message was spread with words and actions, as well as non-verbally. Today people often wear clothing that contains words or symbols which communicate powerful Christian messages. This activity provides instructions for making T-shirts with words and or symbols to help participants communicate the basic message of the Bible: God's Love.

Think about ways to be a missionary—everyday. Consider opportunities to share the message of God's love at home, at school, at church, and in the community. Select words and symbols which represent these actions. Now, create a T-shirt containing these mission messages.

Select a piece of paper and a pencil. Write and draw the words and symbols on it. If words are used, be sure that the letters are written in reverse. Color the designs with fabric crayons. Use solid, steady strokes and outline each letter in a dark color.

Bring the T-shirt and the artwork to the person in charge of the ironing station. Position the front of the shirt over the board and place the colored paper face-down on the cloth. Cover the design with brown paper. Iron the design into the fabric using a slow, firm, steady motion. The iron must be very hot for the design to transfer properly. Carefully remove the paper from the shirt.

Wear the shirt and remember that you are a missionary entrusted with spreading the good news of Jesus' love.

Enhancements

Although the information and ideas contained in Bible Basics are suggested for use in a Learning Center format, the contents and concepts can be easily adapted for use in various worship, education, nurture, and outreach settings within a congregation. Try the suggestions for twelve areas of ministry and modify the material and methods to meet specific situations and circumstances.

Adult Bible Study

- Research and report on the customs and culture of the time period in which Biblical events took place.

- Study a "Book of the Bible" a month using historical and contemporary interpretations of its contents.

Children's Church/Worship

- Create a children's bulletin to introduce basic information about the Bible.

- Introduce the children to a Scripture story by reading it from various translations of the Bible.

Confirmation Classes

- Emphasize the use of Bible study tools such as atlases, commentaries, concordances, and dictionaries.

- Interview members of the church staff and of the congregation and ask them to name their favorite Scripture passages and to share why they are important in their lives.

Intergenerational Events

- Depict the "Sequence" of "How did we get the Bible" in a series of "Living Tableaus," a representation of a scene by an individual or a group dressed in costume.

- Highlight information about authors of the Books of the Bible in a "This Is Your Life" format.

Outreach

- Become involved in a local, regional, national or international project that emphasizes Bible distribution and translation.

- Emphasize ways of sharing the Bible's message of God's love with the hungry, thirsty, stranger, poor, sick, and imprisoned.

Retreats

- Hold an annual "Bible Basics" retreat for third graders to introduce them to the organization and use of the Bible.

- Show a series of videos on the process of producing the Bible and on specific books and themes.

Sunday School

- Make a mural highlighting a theme, key verse, or favorite story from each book of the Bible.

- Teach ways to learn the names of the books of the Bible in sequence.

Vacation Bible School

- Design a Vacation Bible School program on "Bible Basics."

- Integrate the Learning Center activities into a Bible times setting.

Week Day Programs—After School Care And Kid's Clubs

- Organize an Art Exhibit of items created in the Learning Centers.

- Present a program, such as a puppet show, illustrating favorite Bible stories and themes.

Women's & Men's Groups

- Begin a mentoring program between adults and young people and commit to helping students apply God's Word to life situations.

- Invite a speaker to address the topic of archeological expeditions and Bible translation.

Worship

- Construct a series of banners depicting the importance of the Bible.

- Participate in "Bible Sunday".

Youth Groups

- Design a series of games to teach information about the sections of the Old and New Testaments.

- Produce a video to share information on the process of translating the Hebrew Old Testament and the Greek New Testament into English.

CHART OF THE ENGLISH BIBLE

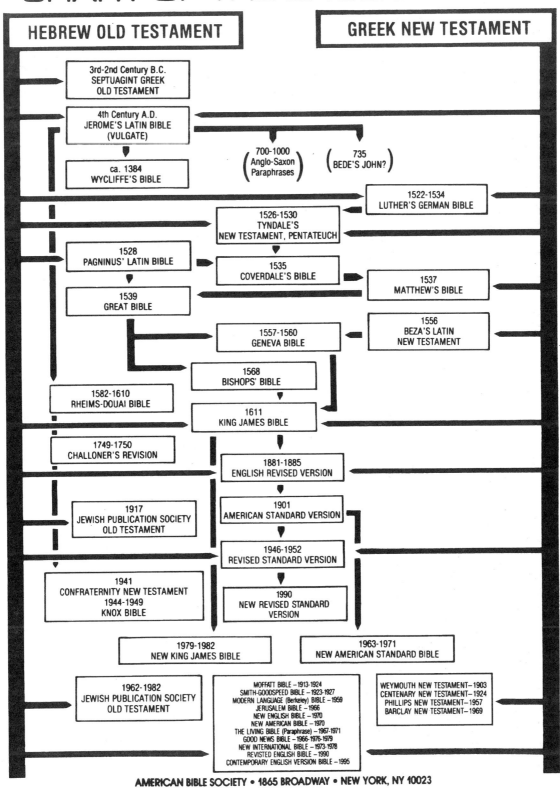

HEBREW OLD TESTAMENT

GREEK NEW TESTAMENT

3rd-2nd Century B.C.
SEPTUAGINT GREEK
OLD TESTAMENT

4th Century A.D.
JEROME'S LATIN BIBLE
(VULGATE)

ca. 1384
WYCLIFFE'S BIBLE

700-1000
Anglo-Saxon
Paraphrases

735
BEDE'S JOHN?

1522-1534
LUTHER'S GERMAN BIBLE

1526-1530
TYNDALE'S
NEW TESTAMENT, PENTATEUCH

1528
PAGNINUS' LATIN BIBLE

1535
COVERDALE'S BIBLE

1537
MATTHEW'S BIBLE

1539
GREAT BIBLE

1557-1560
GENEVA BIBLE

1556
BEZA'S LATIN
NEW TESTAMENT

1568
BISHOPS' BIBLE

1582-1610
RHEIMS-DOUAI BIBLE

1611
KING JAMES BIBLE

1749-1750
CHALLONER'S REVISION

1881-1885
ENGLISH REVISED VERSION

1917
JEWISH PUBLICATION SOCIETY
OLD TESTAMENT

1901
AMERICAN STANDARD VERSION

1946-1952
REVISED STANDARD VERSION

1941
CONFRATERNITY NEW TESTAMENT
1944-1949
KNOX BIBLE

1990
NEW REVISED STANDARD
VERSION

1979-1982
NEW KING JAMES BIBLE

1963-1971
NEW AMERICAN STANDARD BIBLE

1962-1982
JEWISH PUBLICATION SOCIETY
OLD TESTAMENT

MOFFATT BIBLE – 1913-1924
SMITH-GOODSPEED BIBLE – 1923-1927
MODERN LANGUAGE (Berkeley) BIBLE – 1959
JERUSALEM BIBLE – 1966
NEW ENGLISH BIBLE – 1970
NEW AMERICAN BIBLE – 1970
THE LIVING BIBLE (Paraphrase) – 1967-1971
GOOD NEWS BIBLE – 1966-1976-1979
NEW INTERNATIONAL BIBLE – 1973-1978
REVISED ENGLISH BIBLE – 1990
CONTEMPORARY ENGLISH VERSION BIBLE – 1995

WEYMOUTH NEW TESTAMENT – 1903
CENTENARY NEW TESTAMENT – 1924
PHILLIPS NEW TESTAMENT – 1957
BARCLAY NEW TESTAMENT – 1969

AMERICAN BIBLE SOCIETY • 1865 BROADWAY • NEW YORK, NY 10023

[3]American Bible Society. "Chart Of The English Bible." New York: American Bible Society, 1997. Used by permission.

NOTES FOR THE NOTEBOOK

Greek Septuagint: The Old Testament was translated into Greek during the third and second centuries B.C. for Jews living outside of Palestine. The name "Septuagint" (Latin for 70) reflects the tradition that it was translated in Egypt by 70 elders in 70 sessions. It became the Bible of the first generation of Christians to evangelize the Hellenistic world.

Greek New Testament: Paul wrote his letters for the early Christians in Greek. Aramaic was the language spoken by Jesus, but the whole New Testament was written in Greek, the language of the Mediterranean world. By the end of the second century the Old and New Testaments in Greek were used by the church as a special group of sacred writings.

Vulgate Bible: About 382 the Bishop of Rome asked Jerome to prepare a Latin translation of the Bible. Jerome's translation came to be called the Vulgate or "common" Bible. It served as the official text for the Roman Catholic Church from the Council of Trent to the Second Vatican Council.

Bede: Bede, the great historian of Anglo-Saxon England, began to translate portions of the Latin Vulgate Bible into the English of his day, because only the scholars could understand Latin. Legend says that he died as he was finishing the translation of the Gospel of John in 735. In the 10th and 11th centuries other translations were made of the Psalms and the Gospels.

Wycliffe: John Wycliffe led a movement of poor priests, called Lollards, who preached to the people in their own language instead of the Latin used in the churches. He realized that a Bible in English was needed, and under his inspiration the first translation of the entire Bible into English was made from Latin about 1384.

Luther: The Reformaton brought a renewed demand for the Bible in the language of the people. Luther himself prepared the German translation (New Testament 1522, Old Testament 1534). This was the first western European Bible not based on the Latin Vulgate, but on the original Hebrew and Greek texts.

Tyndale: When church authorities in England prohibited a new English translation, Tyndale went to Germany where he translated the New Testament from the original Greek. This first printed English New Testament was published in 1526. Copies were smuggled into England in shipments of grain and cloth, and frequently confiscated. Tyndale also translated portions of the Old Testament (Pentateuch 1530, Jonah 1531). Tyndale was betrayed, strangled and burned near Brussels. His work was so excellent that almost every English version since has been indebted to it.

Coverdale: Coverdale, like Tyndale, fled to Germany to complete a translation of the Bible. He used Latin and German versions as well as Tyndale's New Testament and portions of the Old Testament. This was the first printed English Bible (1535). Matthew's Bible (1537) contained additional sections of Tyndale's unpublished work (through 2 Chronicles), and portions translated by Coverdale (Ezra to Malachi and the Apocrypha). A revision of Matthew's Bible by Coverdale was known as the Great Bible (1539). The Psalms of the Great Bible underlie the Psalter in the *Book of Common Prayer*. The Bishops' Bible (1568), which was a revision of the Great Bible prepared by Matthew Parker and others, served as the base for the revision ordered by King James . The Geneva Bible (1560), also a revision of the Great Bible, was produced by English Puritans in Geneva; it was dependent on the Latin texts of Pagninus' Old Testament (1528) and Beza's New Testament (1556), and exerted a strong influence on the King James Bible.

King James: The various versions of the Bible aroused so many arguments that James I, after the Hampton Court Conference, appointed 54 scholars to make a new version. It took about seven years to complete the work, a monument to the critical scholarship of the time. Despite the great variety of the men who worked on it, the translation was harmonious in style and beauty. It was first published in 1611, and soon became the most popular English Bible.

Roman Catholic Versions: The New Testament published in Rheims (1582) and the Old Testament in Douai (1609-1610) were translated from the Latin Vulgate. These were revised by Bishop Challoner in 1749 and 1750. Ronald A. Knox prepared an independent translation of the Latin Vulgate text into modern English usage (New Testament 1944, Bible 1949). The Confraternity New Testament (1941) was also based on the Vulgate text, but it was influenced by Greek critical editions as well. When a new translation of the Old Testament, based on the Hebrew text, was completed in 1970, it was published with a revision of the 1941 New Testament based on the Greek text, as the New American Bible. Meanwhile the Jerusalem Bible (1966), edited by A. Jones, was a fresh critical translation with notes, inspired by the French *Bible de Jérusalem* (1954).

Later Revisions and Translations: For more than 250 years the King James Bible was supreme among English-speaking people. During the last 100 years, the knowledge from newly-discovered manuscripts, archeological discoveries and recent scholarship has led to its revision. The first "Revised Version" was published in England (1881-1885); a modification of this English Revised Version, the American Standard Version, was issued in 1901. Modern-speech versions of the early 20th century include those by Richard F. Weymouth (New Testament 1903), James Moffatt (New Testament 1913, Bible 1924), J.M.P. Smith and E.J. Goodspeed (New Testament 1923, Bible 1927), and Helen Barrett Montgomery (Centenary New Testament 1924). The last three decades have been characterized by an increase in the number of Bible translations. The Jewish Publication Society has revised its 1917 Old Testament with a new translation of the Torah (1962), the Prophets (1978), and the Writings (1982). Modern-speech versions of the New Testament include those of J.B. Phillips (1957, revised 1972), who also translated portions of the Prophets (1963), and William Barclay (1969). Complete Bibles include the Revised Standard Version (New Testament 1946, second edition 1971, Bible 1952), the Modern Language (Berkeley) Bible (New Testament 1945, Bible 1959, revised 1969), the New English Bible (New Testament 1961, Bible 1970), the Jerusalem Bible (1966), the New American Bible (1970), New American Standard Bible (1971), the Living Bible, a paraphrase (New Testament 1967, Bible 1971), the Good News Bible (New Testament 1966, Bible 1976, Apocrypha 1979), the New International Version (New Testament 1973, Bible 1978), the New King James Version (New Testament 1979, Bible 1982), the New Revised Standard Version Bible, 1990, and the Contemporary English Version (New Testament 1991, Bible 1995).

Printed in the United States of America
Chart of Eng. Bible-102987
ABS-2/97-500-2,800—ES4

Supplements Intergenerational Learning[4]

Intergenerational programming is not a new concept. The church has been "intergenerational" long before it was politically correct. Literally, "intergenerational" means between or among the ages. In other words, anything is "intergenerational" when people of all ages or a mixed age group work and learn together. The church is an ideal place for this kind of learning environment because all members should see themselves as children of God, sharing faith in common.

All churches already have built-in intergenerational programs, the largest and most obvious being worship. Dinners, church family fellowship times, special celebrations, and experiential vacation Bible schools are all places where groups are mixed and learning occurs across age boundaries. The place where churches frequently fail to implement such important cross-graded groupings is in the Christian education program.

There are many reasons why intergenerational experiences are important to include in Christian education settings. First and foremost is that learning across age groups helps build one of the most important aspects of faith development: relationships. When grandparents and their grandchildren are helping each other learn a Biblical story, they are also learning about each other. They are passing on a faith tradition through mentoring and modeling that is mutually beneficial. Even among participants who are not genetically related, working together on a project helps to break down artificial barriers of prejudice about age. In mixed age groups, we learn that everyone has something to contribute and that we can all learn from one another. The experts tell us that children (and adults) will remember as much as 90% of what they teach to someone else. Jesus appreciated the value of intergenerational learning, welcoming all who came to Him and involving them in the lesson. How else could He have taken a child on His lap to teach the disciples?

The key is to purposefully plan to include a variety of ages in at least some of the learning experiences that occur at church. Certain seasonal events or specific times of the year—such as summer Sunday school—lend themselves well to intergenerational learning. The people in charge of such events must, however, be sure that programs are not haphazardly put together. It is essential that planning be done well in advance with input from all age groups involved. Be clear about what objectives for learning are intended; make sure all directions are well thought out and clear instructions are given. Involve as many people as possible with specific tasks to help the event occur.

Certain elements help to ensure success for any experience. First, be sure to include a "get-acquainted" activity, something to break down "cliques" or to prevent people from age-grouping themselves. One good way to avoid these pitfalls is to pre-assign cooperative partners or groups, or to use a random method of assigning groups that will better assure mixed pairings. A good design for facilitating learning in cross-graded groupings is the use of learning centers or rotation models. Develop areas of discovery around topics so that pairs or groups can move from one center to another, exploring the lesson from a variety of shared experiences. Take time to celebrate the learning that occurs with food and fun, closing whenever possible with a large group sharing of the learning experiences.

[4] Used by permission. Liechty, Anna L. and Phyllis Vos Wezeman. Church Seasons, Vol. 1, number 3. (Mishawaka, IN: Active Learning Associates, Inc.) March 1997.

Supplements Learning Activities Used In Bible Basics

Activities contained in <u>Bible Basics</u> are cross-referenced by method. The phrase listed below each activity indicates the chapter where it may be found and the words in parenthesis indicate the section of the chapter where the activity is located.

Art

- ■ Bible Cover
  - ● Using The Bible (Supplements)
- ■ Collage
  - ● Sharing The Bible (Project Possibilities)
- ■ Cross Bookmark
  - ● Using The Bible (Cross References)
- ■ Definition Device
  - ● Studying The Bible (Bible Dictionary)
- ■ Graffiti Chalkboard
  - ● What Is The Bible? (What is the Bible?)
- ■ Key Mobile
  - ● Studying The Bible (Concordance)
- ■ Magnet
  - ● Sharing The Bible (Magnet)
- ■ Matchbox Books
  - ● What Is The Bible? (What are the books of the Bible?)
- ■ Mobile
  - ● The New Testament (History)
- ■ Paper Chain
  - ● Producing The Bible (Books Of The Bible Review)
- ■ Paper Making
  - ● Producing The Bible (Writing Surfaces)
- ■ Punctuation Pin
  - ● Using The Bible (Book, Chapter, And Verse)
- ■ Scroll
  - ● The Old Testament (Law)

■ Spatter Painted Bookmark
  ● What Is The Bible? (Why is the Bible important?)
■ Stamp Printing
  ● Producing The Bible (Printing Processes)
■ Tangram
  ● The New Testament (Gospels)
■ T-shirt
  ● Sharing The Bible (T-Shirt Themes)

Dance

■ Macarena
  ● Sharing The Bible (Dance Directions)

Creative Writing

■ Acrostic Poem
  ● The Old Testament (Poetry)
■ Poem
  ● Studying The Bible (Commentary)
■ Diamond Shaped Poem
  ● The New Testament (Prophecy)

Games

■ Atlas Study
  ● Studying The Bible (Atlas Study)
■ Board Game
  ● Using The Bible (Versions Of The Bible)
■ Clothespin Game
  ● The New Testament (Epistles)
■ Code
  ● Producing The Bible (Language Systems)
■ Crossword Puzzle
  ● What Is The Bible? (What are the parts of the Bible?)
■ "Go Fish" Game
  ● The New Testament (New Testament Review)
■ Lotto Game
  ● Using The Bible (Book Names And Abbreviations)
■ Magnetic Sequencing Game
  ● The Old Testament (Prophets)
■ Matching Game
  ● Producing The Bible (Translating Techniques)
■ Sequencing Sheets
  ● What Is The Bible? (How did we get the Bible?)
■ Spinner Game
  ● The Old Testament (Old Testament Review)
■ Tic Toe Game
  ● The Old Testament (History)

■ Two-part Puzzle
  ● Studying The Bible (Books Of The Bible Review)

Puppets

■ Spoon Puppet
  ● Sharing The Bible (Story Spoons)

Additional Learning Activity Suggestions

Since the lessons in <u>Bible Basics</u> were designed for use in Learning Centers, activities focus on methods that adapt to individual and small group projects. Although art, creative writing, and games have been emphasized, there are many additional methods to incorporate into lesson plans. Try the suggestions provided and use them as springboards to develop additional learning activities.

Architecture

● Design a "Scavenger Hunt" to look for Biblical themes in the architecture of the church building—inside and outside.

● Explore the topic of archeology and set up a simulated "dig" in the classroom.

Art

● Build a table-top model depicting one scene from a Biblical, Historical, or Contemporary time period.

● Make masks to represent the faces of people and use them to help tell the story.

Banners/Textiles

● Design a banner depicting the theme of each book of the Bible.

● Sew a costume and represent one of the characters highlighted during a session.

Computers

● Locate software on Biblical themes.

● Search the Internet using key words and phrases from the chapters of <u>Bible Basics</u>.

Creative Writing

● Use a variety of poetry forms to summarize the message of the Bible.

● Write a description of events from the point of view of one of the people in a lesson.

Culinary

- Hold an all church supper featuring foods representing various Bible stories.
- Recreate a feast like one shared in Bible times.

Dance

- Add gestural interpretation as a Scripture passage is read.
- Learn sign language to interpret songs that communicate the basic message of the Bible.

Drama

- Create a tableau to depict the process of producing the Bible.
- Perform a first-person monologue to share a story.

Games

- Choose a favorite game format (Concentration, Password, etc.) and adapt it to teach the books of the Bible.
- Devise "Bingo" cards with the names of the books of the Bible.

Music

- Perform a musical celebrating the Bible as God's Word.
- Use familiar tunes to make up songs about people in the stories.

Photography

- Create a photo essay illustrating the theme "Sharing The Bible" locally, regionally, nationally, and internationally.
- Review resource books containing photos of "Bible Basics" themes and stories.

Puppetry

- Draw a figure of a person on a piece of cardboard or posterboard. Cut out holes for the head and the arms and put yourself in the picture.
- Write a puppet script to accompany the theme of each chapter.

Storytelling

- Associate an object with each book and talk about the Bible from that perspective.
- Re-tell a Bible story using a "round robin" approach, with each person adding 3 to 5 words to the narrative.

Supplements
Learning Centers

A Learning Center may be defined as the focal point of activity for the purpose of acquiring knowledge or skill. It must contain information on a topic and instructions for a task as well as supplies and equipment necessary to complete an activity or an assignment. Designed especially for individual students, learning centers also work well for small group projects.

Learning Centers may be created on tabletops, desks, counters, bulletin boards, chalk boards, walls, floors, or any other surface that will hold the essential elements. Learning Centers may be extremely efficient, containing the bare essentials required for achieving the desired results, or extraordinarily elaborate with bountiful enhancements to supplement the anticipated outcomes.

Learning Centers create an opportunity for the learning to occur; develop discovery learning techniques; emphasize hands-on experiences; focus attention on specific topics and tasks; foster cooperative learning; promote critical thinking skills; provide self-directed, individualized instruction; release imagination and ideas.

To use the five lessons in each chapter of <u>Bible Basics</u> as Learning Centers, duplicate the information and instructions for each activity, gather the supplies, complete the advance preparation, create an example, and place the materials in an appropriate location. Students may be self-directed, may work in pairs or small groups, or may have an adult facilitate the process at each Center. Each class could begin and end with a large group time to introduce the theme of the session, to provide instructions for the process, and to facilitate a time of closure and evaluation.

Supplements Learning Styles/Multiple Intelligences

"Learning Styles" is not a new concept in Christian education. Teachers have known for years that students learn in different ways—especially through auditory, visual, and kinesthetic experiences. An anonymous quote reminds the educator that people learn by hearing, seeing, and doing: "I hear—I forget; I see—I remember; I do—I understand."

Because of recent work by Howard Gardner, Educational Research Professor at Harvard Graduate School of Education, the buzz word for "Learning Styles" has become "Multiple Intelligences." Gardner suggests that each person possesses seven "intelligences."[5]

Bodily/Kinesthetic

Description

The capacity to use one's whole body to express ideas and feelings and the facility to use one's hands to produce or transform things.

Learns Best By

Becoming physically involved with the information to be learned. Needs to move or manipulate objects to have a successful learning experience. Too much sitting or inactivity will cause this student to tune out.

Teaching Activities

- Art and crafts
- Dancing, signing, sports
- Drama, motions, pantomime, puppets, role-play
- Physical activities

Interpersonal/Relational

Description

The ability to perceive and make distinctions in the moods, intentions, motivation, and feelings of other people. Sensitivity to facial expressions, voice and gestures. Motivation and learning stem from cooperative learning tasks and bouncing ideas off others. Prefers to work with others on a project or shared study.

Learns Best By

Talking with others. Cooperative or paired learning is how this student flourishes. Is stifled by introspection and long periods of silent study.

Teaching Activities

- Answering questions
- Brainstorming ideas
- Comparing and contrasting ideas
- Cooperative learning in groups
- Interviews, discussion, and dialogue
- Playing cooperative games

Interpersonal/Introspective

Description

The ability to act adaptively on the basis of self-knowledge. Being aware of one's inner moods, intentions, motivations, and a capacity for self-understanding.

Learns Best By

Working alone on projects. Will choose to reflect and be self-directed in their learning paths.

Teaching Activities

- Emotional processing
- Focus on inner feelings, meditation
- Identifying with characters in a story
- Research projects
- Silent reflection, centering and inward journey
- Thinking strategies
- Working alone

Linguistic/Verbal

Description

The capacity to use words effectively, orally or in writing.

Learns Best By

Saying things aloud, hearing words spoken, and seeing words in print. Words are tools to be used in learning. Becomes frustrated with verbal stimulation and challenging concepts.

Teaching Activities

- Completing sentences
- Debate
- Memorizing dates, names, and trivia
- Reading and telling stories
- Writing litanies, poems, and stories

Logical/Mathematical

Description

The capacity to use numbers effectively and to reason well. This includes sensitivity to logical patterns and relationships.

Learns Best By

Categorizing and classifying things. Rational thinking is the primary tool used in learning. Finds it difficult to function in arenas of confusion or chaos, too much repetition, and unspecified goals.

Teaching Activities

- Codes
- Experiments working with numbers and math
- Exploring patterns and relationships
- Games
- Number and word puzzles
- Problem solving and sequencing

Musical/Rhythmic

Description

The capacity to perceive, discriminate, transform, and express musical forms.

Learns Best By

Using rhythm, melody, and music combined with the information to be learned. Enjoys being surrounded by sound and rhythm and understands these as learning tools. Long reading or writing assignments, lectures, and large amounts of seat work is boring and causes stress to this type of learner.

Teaching Activities

- Bible verses set to music
- Humming, singing, and listening to music
- Learning hymns and musicals
- Listening to and learning story songs
- Making and playing instruments
- Writing new words to familiar tunes
- Writing or performing musical compositions

Visual/Spatial

Description

The ability to perceive the visual-spatial world accurately and to perform transformations upon those perceptions. It includes the capacity to visualize, to graphically represent visual or spatial ideas.

Learns Best By

Visualizing and dreaming about concepts and ideas. Pictures are tools to enhance learning. Too much printed material and too much writing will frustrate and discourage learning.

Teaching Activities

- Art activities in various media
- Designing and building models
- Drawing, painting and sculpting
- Graphs, maps, pictures and puzzles
- Pretending, guided imagery, and visualization
- Studying symbols and using charts and posters

It is important to remember that the seven ways of knowing, the multiple intelligences, are interconnected. Each person has preferred ways of learning, but the best learning takes place when the student experiences learning in all seven ways.[6]

[5]Gardner, Howard. Frames of Mind: The Theory of Multiple Intelligences. Basic Books, 1983, 1985.

[6]Bruce, Barbara. 7 Ways of Teaching the Bible to Children. (Nashvile, TN: Abingdon Press) 1997.

Supplements
Lesson Planning[7]

In secular education the name Madeline Hunter has become synonymous with a five-step method of instructional design proven to increase student mastery of new material. In religious education, teachers can adapt and apply this method to aid Biblical learners of all ages. The method consists of five basic steps that most teachers already recognize are a part of any well-planned lesson. Formalizing and following the procedure simply assures that each time a teacher prepares he or she will intentionally design each step, and thus increase the opportunities for student success.

Lesson Objective

Before a lesson can ever be taught, the leader must determine what is the intended outcome for the students. What will they be able to do after they have received this new information and have participated in the planned experience? The best learning occurs when the objective is specific and clear—both to the teacher and to the student. Once the teacher has determined the focus for her or his efforts, then the five steps of the lesson plan can guide as he or she designs the learning process.

Step One—Introduction: Transition And Anticipatory Set

It is the teacher's responsibility to help prepare the students mentally for the new learning. This phase should be kept short so that there is enough time available for instruction and practice, but it is essential to get the lesson off to a good start by transitioning from previous learning to the new message and by setting a meaningful context for students to transfer their earlier knowledge to the new situation. Once the learners develop ownership of the story, then they are more likely to learn and remember the new layers of information introduced to them.

Step Two—Instruction: Providing Information, Modeling, Checking For Understanding, Structured Practice

The teacher must determine what background knowledge is essential for students to understand and then provide that necessary information. Simple details may need to be communicated. Use as many ways of modeling the information as possible. After the essentials have been communicated, the teacher asks specific questions to determine if students understand or if more explanation and/or modeling is needed. If students can answer straightforward questions, and the teacher feels the information is mastered, then it is time for structured practice.

In structured practice, all students participate while the teacher monitors responses and gives specific feedback.

Step Three—Guided Practice

When the students have achieved mastery of structured practice—at least 80% can answer questions correctly and comprehend the lesson—the teacher provides opportunities for students to practice their newly found information. The teachers role would be to guide and offer help, but it is important to let the students practice their learning individually or in small groups and to share the results with one another.

Step Four—Closure And Summary

A final review sums up and brings a closure to the learning effort. The leader should return to the original goal and have the students participate in an activity to bring the lesson to its conclusion.

Step Five—Independent Practice

The need for follow-up activities remains until students have achieved sufficient mastery to use their new knowledge on their own. Future practice could include presenting their guided practice projects for other groups, for example younger children's classes or older adults.

The effective teacher, whether in a religious education or a public school classroom, is one whose students learn that which was intended. True, the Holy Spirit can inspire us in unplanned ways, but God's ordered universe and the masterful plan devised to bring salvation are sufficient examples to us of the need to plan ahead and to bring the youth in our charge the best we have to share.

---

[7] Used by permission. Liechty, Anna L. And Phyllis Vos Wezeman. Church Season, Vol. 2, Number 2. (Mishawaka, IN: Active Learning Associates, Inc.) November 1997.

Supplements
Workshop Rotation Model

Workshop Rotation is a model for Christian Education programming, especially adaptable to an instructional design for Sunday School. The concept revolves around a posted schedule of students—or classes—rotating into a new lesson—the workshop—focusing on the same story for a designated number of weeks. In other words, leaders prepare one "lesson" and teach it to different groups of students each week for four to six weeks. Students, who remain in small groups organized by age group or mixed age groups, move from workshop to workshop to experience the same story in a different way during each week of the rotation period. Although rooms, or "workshops", may be called by different names they usually include an Art Studio, a Drama/Puppetry Room, a Music Room, a Game Room, an Audio/Video Room, and a Computer room.

Each Chapter of the book Bible Basics may be used in a Workshop Rotation Model. Simply start with the five learning activities provided and add or adapt additional resources. For example, find a video to enhance the theme, locate music that teaches the message, and boot up computer programs on the topic. Many additional options are possible. This Multiple Intelligences approach provides opportunities for students to experience the message of God's Word through active participation.

Resources

The following resources—as well as many others—have been and are being used in conjunction with the development of the series Bible Basics. They may aid lesson preparation for teachers and students.

Blankenbaker, Frances, Editor. What The Bible Is All About For Young Explorers. Ventura, CA: Regal Books, 1986.

Coleman, Lyman, Editor. The Serendipity Bible For Study Groups. Grand Rapids, MI: Zondervan, 1989.

———. The NIV Serendipity Bible Study Book. Grand Rapids, MI: Zondervan, 1986.

Davidson, James E. The Year Of The Bible. A Comprehensive, Congregation-Wide Program Of Bible Reading. Participant's Book. Louisville, KY: Bridge Resources, 1996.

Doney, Meryl. How The Bible Came To Us. Oxford, England: Lion Publishing, 1985.

Editors. The Bible And You. South Deerfield, MA: Channing L. Bete Company, 1971.

Editors. The Bible Visual Resource Book For Do-It-Yourself Bible Scholars. Ventura, CA: Regal Books, 1989.

Editors. How The Bible Came To Be. South Deerfield, MA: Channing L. Bete Company, 1975.

———. How To Study The Bible. South Deerfield, MA: Channing L. Bete Company, 1978.

Editors. Life Application Bible. New Revised Standard Version. Iowa Falls, IA: World Bible Publishers, 1990.

Editors. What You Should Know About The New Testament. South Deerfield, MA: Channing L. Bete Company, 1988.

———. What You Should Know About The Old Testament. South Deerfield, MA: Channing L. Bete Company, 1988.

Ferguson, Duncan S. Bible Basics: Mastering The Content Of The Bible. Louisville, KY: Westminster John Knox Press, 1995.

Flood, Robert G. 30-Minute Panorama Of The Bible. Chicago, IL: Moody Press, 1984.

Goodspeed, Edgar J. The Story Of The Bible. Chicago, IL: University of Chicago Press.

Halley, Henry H. Halley's Bible Handbook. Grand Rapids, MI: , 1962 (Twenty-Third Printing).

Harold, Betty Sharp. A Bird's-Eye View Of The Bible From Genesis To Revelation. Louisville, KY: Bridge Resources, 1996.

Heim, Ralph D. Reader's Companion To The Bible. Philadelphia, PA: Fortress Press, 1975.

Hill, Andrew E., Compiler. Baker's Handbook Of Bible Lists. Grand Rapids, MI: Baker Book House, 1981.

Jacobson, Diane L. and Robert Kyar. A Beginner's Guide To The Books Of The Bible. Minneapolis, MN: Augsburg, 1991.

Lockyer, Herbert. All The Books And Chapters Of The Bible. Grand Rapids, MI: Zondervan, 1966.

Lucado, Max, Editor. The Inspirational Study Bible. Dallas, TX: Word Bibles, 1995.

Mears, Henrietta C. What The Bible Is All About. Glendale, CA: Regal Books, 1966.

Minges, Barbara. The Bible: Our Book Of Faith. Pittsburgh, PA: The Logos System Associates, 1988.

———. Investigator's Notebook. The Bible: Our Book Of Faith. Pittsburgh, PA: The Logos System Associates, 1988.

Richards, Lawrence. International Children's Bible Handbook. Fort Worth, TX: Worthy Publishing, 1986.

Schuessler, Paul. Bible Reading Handbook. Minneapolis, MN: Bible Reading Handbook, 1991.

Shortwell, Berenice Myers. Getting Better Acquainted With Your Bible. Kennebunkport, ME: Shadwold Press, 1972.

Trefzer, John D. Reading The Bible With Understanding. St. Louis, MO: Bethany Press, 1978.

Wright, Chris. User's Guide To The Bible. Tring, , England: Lion Publishing, 1984.

Additional Resources

Reference Books

Review reference books such as Atlases, Bible Story books, Bibles (various translations,) Commentaries, Concordances, Dictionaries, and Encyclopedias.

Groups

Contact Bible Societies, Denominational Offices, Mission Agencies, and Translation Organizations. Also contact College, Seminary, and University Departments of Archeology, Religion, and Theology.

Internet

Search electronic retrieval systems using key words related to topics.

Plans For Future Books In The <u>Bible Basics</u> Series Include:

<u>Bible Basics: The Old Testament—Genesis Through Esther</u>

<u>Bible Basics: The Old Testament—Job Through Malachi</u>

<u>Bible Basics: The New Testament—Matthew Through Revelation</u>